ABRAHAM JOSHUA HESCHEL

MODERN SPIRITUAL MASTERS SERIES

ABRAHAM JOSHUA HESCHEL

Essential Writings

Selected with an Introduction by

SUSANNAH HESCHEL

ORBIS BOOKS

Maryknoll, New York 10545

Thirteenth Printing, April 2022

Founded in 1970, Orbis Books endeavors to publish works that enlighten the mind, nourish the spirit, and challenge the conscience. The publishing arm of the Mary-knoll Fathers and Brothers, Orbis seeks to explore the global dimensions of the Christian faith and mission, to invite dialogue with diverse cultures and religious traditions, and to serve the cause of reconciliation and peace. The books published reflect the views of their authors and do not represent the official position of the Maryknoll Society. To learn more about Maryknoll and Orbis Books, please visit our website at www.maryknoll.org.

Manufactured in the United States of America.

Library of Congress Cataloging-in-Publication Data
Heschel, Abraham Joshua, 1907–1972.
　Abraham Joshua Heschel : essential writings / selected with an Introduction by Susannah Heschel.
　　p. cm. – (Modern spiritual masters series)
　　ISBN 978-1-57075-919-2 (pbk.)
　　1. Jewish philosophy–20th century 2. Judaism–20th century. 3. Judaism–Relations–Christianity. 4. Christianity and other religions–Judaism. I. Heschel, Susannah. II. Title.
　B5800.H47 2011
　296.3–dc22　　　　　　　　　　　　　　　　　　　2010050033

*This book is dedicated to
my father's beloved and devoted nieces,*

*Thena Heshel Kendall (London)
and
Pearl Heschel Twersky (New York),*

*who carry forward the brilliance and nobility
of the Heschel family*

Contents

Sources   15

Introduction   17

1. IF YOU WANT TO KNOW GOD,
   SHARPEN YOUR SENSE OF THE HUMAN   45

   To Recover the Questions   49
   Rooster   51
   Wonder   51
   Nature   53
   Embarrassment   54
   The Three Dimensions   56
   The Meaning of Awe   56
   Radical Amazement   58

2. PROPHECY IS THE VOICE THAT GOD
   HAS LENT TO THE SILENT AGONY   60

   What Manner of Man Is the Prophet?   62
   Telegram to President John F. Kennedy   64
   Religion and Race   65
   To Despair Is to Betray   75
   After Majdanek   76
   our Afterlife   77
   Kaddish for Our Souls   78
   Prayer for Soviet Jews   80
   Introduction to Martin Luther King at Riverside   81
   Introduction to Martin Luther King at Concord   83
   Toward a Just Society: Prayer   84
   What Is Sin?   85

3. GOD IS NOT SILENT.
    HE HAS BEEN SILENCED   88

        The Hiding God   89
        God Follows Me Everywhere   93
        God Is the Subject   93
        Faith Is an Event   94
        Prayer as Discipline   95
        On Prayer   100

4. IN THE REALM OF SPIRIT ONLY HE
    WHO IS A PIONEER IS ABLE TO BE AN HEIR   102

        Faith as an Individual Memory   105
        Dissent   106
        The Spirit of Judaism   107
        Existence and Celebration   108
        Yom Kippur   110
        Education   112
        Rabbis   114
        No Religion Is an Island   116

5. PRAYER MAKES US WORTHY OF BEING SAVED   137

        The Ability to Answer   139
        On Prayer: Young People   143
        Beyond Faith   146
        Out of the Depth We Cry for Help   149
        The Sabbath   150
        Celebration   154
        The Vocation of the Cantor   158
        Preach in Order to Pray   167

6. GOD IS OF NO IMPORTANCE
    UNLESS HE IS OF SUPREME IMPORTANCE   169

        Why I Had to Write This Book   171
        In Praise of Strict Justice   174

Religious Truth Must Be Lived	175
From the Point of View of God	179
Some of Us Blush	184
Man's Relevance to God	187
What to Do with Wonder	188
Our Destiny Is to Aid	189

Acknowledgments

For his devoted attention to this book and for his superb staff at Orbis Books, I want to express my gratitude to my editor, Robert Ellsberg. I am delighted and honored that he asked me to edit this volume of my father's writings for the distinguished Spiritual Masters series he edits at Orbis Books and for the ongoing conversation we have had as I worked with him on this project. With this book my father joins company with some of the outstanding spiritual thinkers of his day who are part of the Orbis series, including some who were friends of his: Martin Buber, Thomas Merton, Dorothy Day, and Daniel Berrigan.

I would also like to thank Maria Angelini and Catherine Costello, both at Orbis Books, for their careful editing of the manuscript.

Most of the writings included in this volume were published by my father during his lifetime, but a few appear in print for the first time. They are fragments of his handwritten manuscripts that I have found among his papers, and I am grateful for the insightful treasures they contain.

One of those fragments comes from a speech my father delivered in 1963 to a meeting of the United Synagogue of America, where he spoke, together with Martin Luther King Jr. on the need to rescue Soviet Jewry. I want to thank Helen and Norman Schutzman, who were present that evening, for giving me a copy of the recording of the speeches. My father concluded his lecture with brief remarks on the Holocaust, "Kaddish for Our Souls." He spoke in those final three minutes in a very moving Yiddish, and that Yiddish speech is translated here by my wonderful friend Sylvia Fuks Fried, who has a profound sensitivity to my father's spirit. Moved by his extraordinary

Yiddish, she took great care in preparing a beautiful translation. This was a rare moment in which my father spoke about
an event and its consequences that were terribly painful for him
to discuss in public.

In his superb English translation of one of my father's Yiddish poems, "God Follows Me Everywhere," written when
my father was a student, Jeffrey Shandler, a scholar of Yiddish literature, has captured the delicacy and beauty of my
father's language. I am grateful for his permission to print his
translation in this volume.

For our many long conversations and their very helpful
advice about the conceptualization of this book, my introduction, and the particular excerpts to include, I am fortunate
for the friendship of the monks of Weston Priory (Vermont),
the Catholic theologian Padraic O'Hare, and Rabbi William
Hamilton. My friend Henry F. Smith has given me thoughtful,
insightful responses to my writing about my father for which
I am deeply grateful. Jessica Benjamin has been an extraordinary friend to me and my family and my confidant on matters
academic as well as personal. To her and to my other wonderful New York friends who enrich my life, I thank you for
great conversations, celebrations, and commemorations, and
for honoring my father with your spirits: Margrit Rustow,
Alison Bernstein, Eric Greenberg, Peter Geffen, and the Bnai
Jeshurun rabbis and congregation.

My beloved family — my father's nieces, nephews, and
cousins, members of the Kopitznitzer, Novominsker, Boyaner,
and Chotiner Hasidic dynasties: among you my father's spirit is
nurtured — I thank you with a full heart.

Most of all, I am thrilled to spend my life with Yaakov Aron-
son and thank him for his warmth, love, and great humor. For
their sweetness and charm as well as their cheerful attentiveness at their mother's lectures, I thank our wonderful daughters,
Gittel and Avigael.

I am very grateful to Shuqin Cui, professor at Bowdoin College, for inviting me to her beautiful home in Maine for several

days of quiet in the fall of 2010 so that I could write the introduction to this volume.

Jonathan Wilson, director of the Center for the Humanities at Tufts University, has been an extraordinary host to me for over two years during my sabbatical from Dartmouth College, giving me a stimulating intellectual home and a lovely office in which to read and write.

My thanks to Elena Mortara, who organized a superb conference in Rome in December of 2007 honoring my father's hundredth birthday, at which I presented some of the points raised in my introduction to this volume.

Carol Folt, dean of faculty at Dartmouth College (and now provost), has been very generous in her support of my research and writing, for which I am deeply appreciative.

Among my colleagues at Dartmouth College, I want to extend my particular thanks to Meredyth Morley, Phyllis Ford, and Karen de Rosa for their friendship and spirit of generosity, and to Barbara Merrill and Adrian Bellavance, of the Hanover Inn, for helping me manage the hectic pace of a Dartmouth professorship with their warm smiles and arms outstretched to be helpful. I would also like to thank two Dartmouth students for their assistance in preparing the manuscript for press, Tien-Tien Jong and Carsten Hansen.

To all the readers who tell me how moved they are by my father's writings, please know how much you enhance my life with your words and remind me that my father continues to bless us with his legacy.

Most of all, my gratitude goes to two younger scholars of my father's work, Robert Erlewine and Dror Bondi, who consulted with me about which texts to include. They are the two most insightful and sensitive interpreters of my father's thought, and I also want to take particular note of their emulation of my father's integrity and humanity.

Sources

GSM   *God in Search of Man* by Abraham Joshua Heschel. Excerpts reprinted by permission of Farrar, Straus and Giroux, LLC. Copyright © 1955 by Abraham Joshua Heschel. Copyright renewed 1983 by Sylvia Heschel.

IF   *The Insecurity of Freedom* by Abraham Joshua Heschel. Excerpts reprinted by permission of Farrar, Straus and Giroux, LLC. Copyright © 1966 by Abraham Joshua Heschel. Copyright renewed 1994 by Sylvia Heschel.

Israel   *Israel: An Echo of Eternity* by Abraham Joshua Heschel. Excerpts reprinted by permission of Farrar, Straus and Giroux, LLC. Copyright © 1967 by Abraham Joshua Heschel. Copyright renewed 1995 by Sylvia Heschel.

MGSA   *Moral Grandeur and Spiritual Audacity* by Abraham Joshua Heschel. Excerpts reprinted by permission of Farrar, Straus and Giroux, LLC. Copyright © 1996 Sylvia Heschel. Introduction copyright © 1996 by Susannah Heschel.

MNA   *Man Is Not Alone: A Philosophy of Religion* by Abraham Joshua Heschel. Excerpts reprinted by permission of Farrar, Straus and Giroux, LLC. Copyright © 1951 by Abraham J. Heschel. Copyright renewed 1979 by Sylvia Heschel.

MQG   *Man's Quest for God* by Abraham Joshua Heschel (Santa Fe, N.Mex.: Aurora Press, 1998). Excerpts reprinted with permission. Copyright © 1954. All rights reserved.

PFT   *A Passion for Truth* by Abraham Joshua Heschel. Excerpts reprinted by permission of Farrar, Straus and Giroux, LLC. Copyright © 1973 by Sylvia Heschel.

Prophets   *The Prophets* by Abraham Joshua Heschel (New York: HarperCollins, 1962) Excerpts reprinted by permission of HarperCollins.

Introduction

A journalist once asked my father why he had come to a demonstration against the war in Vietnam. "I am here because I cannot pray," my father told him. Confused and a bit annoyed, the journalist asked him, "What do you mean, you can't pray so you come to a demonstration against the war?" And my father replied, "Whenever I open the prayerbook, I see before me images of children burning from napalm."

Indeed, we forfeit the right to pray, my father said, if we are silent about the cruelties committed in our name by our government. In a free society some are guilty but all are responsible. How dare we come before God with our prayers when we commit atrocities against the one image we have of the divine: human beings.

What is it, after all, to pray? "Prayer must never be a citadel for selfish concerns but rather a place for deepening concern over other people's plight." Rather than making us feel reassured, relaxed, and self-satisfied, "prayer is meaningless unless it is subversive" (*MGSA*, 262). Subversive, that is, of our callousness and indifference — for the opposite of good, my father writes, is not evil, but indifference. To be religious is never to be callous or indifferent, never to be self-satisfied; looking at the world from God's perspective means living in the prophetic tradition: to give voice to those who live in silent agony, to eradicate injustice, to emulate God's compassion for human beings.

And that was precisely the sort of person my father was: filled with concern, at times trembling over the atrocities that filled the twentieth century, empathic to the worries of his family, students, and friends. He had a gift for listening and understanding, lifting the burdens from other people's hearts.

17

Often he was sleepless, engulfed by the horrors of the war in Vietnam, by the racism he called an "eye disease" of white Americans, by the plight of Soviet Jews prevented from practicing Judaism.

Yet he always had courage, and he never despaired — despair is forbidden, he used to say; God is everywhere and never gives us a task without also giving us the strength to carry it out. He was a person who knew how to rejoice, how to celebrate his friends and family, and how to create holiness in time. On the Sabbath, the Torah tells us, we are forbidden to light a fire; my father adds that we are also forbidden to light fires of controversy, and so we had no political debates or sad topics in our home on the Sabbath. Holiness is not given to us but is created by us — we make the Sabbath day holy — and my father knew how to create a holy moment. He said, "It takes three things to create a sense of significant being: God, a soul, and a moment. And the three are always present."[1]

Prayer for him was a service of the heart but also a service of the body. Religiosity was not only a private, inward affair, but a public act: marching in Selma, speaking out against the war in Vietnam. When his friend Daniel Berrigan urged him to go to prison as an act of protest against the war, my father responded that he could be more effective by talking to people, changing their political views. Religious commitment had to be constructive and transformative — that was the prophetic message he lived.

Youth in Poland

My father's religious life came from his Hasidic family. Hasidism, a pietistic movement that arose in Eastern Europe in the eighteenth century, echoes in all of my father's writings. The movement was led by rebbes, rabbinical leaders whose position

---

1. Abraham Joshua Heschel, *The Insecurity of Freedom: Essays on Human Existence* (New York: Farrar, Straus & Giroux, 1967), 84.

was inherited, father to son, and whose efforts were not simply to teach, but to inspire and transform their followers, Hasidim. During his adult life, spent in Germany (1927–38) and in the United States (1940–72), his happiest moments seemed to be when we visited the Hasidic rebbes of his family — those who had survived the war — and his most fervent prayers were at the tiny, simple Hasidic synagogues he would seek out.

My father was born into one of the most distinguished families of Hasidic rebbes, royalty in the world of Jewish piety, and he was destined to become such a rebbe. His mother, Rivka Reizl, descended from the famed Rabbi Levi Yitzhak of Berdichev, was known for her piety, and women clustered near her in the synagogue, inspired by her praying. His father, Moshe Mordecai, raised in the large, majestic court of his grandfather, the Ruzhiner rebbe in Sadegora, had become a rebbe in an impoverished neighborhood in Warsaw, Pelzovizna. Childhood was not about toys and games, but study, and my father was recognized as brilliant when he was very young. He was given special tutors hired to teach him traditional rabbinic texts, and also to cultivate his religious life.

When he was only nine years old, my father's father died during the influenza epidemic of 1916, leaving his mother and siblings impoverished. My father used to tell me stories of his family's extreme poverty and, especially, of the terribly cold winters that left his fingers permanently swollen from having been frozen so often.

What transcended their poverty was the religious atmosphere. My father used to say that he grew up surrounded by "people of religious nobility" — a wonderful phrase — and that he always carried them in his heart. He felt the presence of his Hasidic forebears in his life, giving him strength at moments of sadness. "Always remember your ancestors," he used to say to me gently: remember who you are, what you stand for. The teachings of his ancestors were on his lips constantly. He spoke in particular of the Apter Rav, Abraham Joshua Heschel of Apt, his great-grandfather who died in 1825 in Ukraine and was

known as the "Ohev Yisrael," the one who loves the Jewish
people. Exuding warmth and generosity, the Apter's teachings
were frequently about empathy and generosity, healing people
who were depressed, and rejoicing in Sabbath celebrations. Like
his Hasidic forebears, my father turned religious assumptions
upside down. God was not an object of human contemplation.
My father was imbued with wonder at God's subjectivity: it is
not just that we are in search of God, but that God is in search
of us, in need of us. We are objects of divine concern. We speak
of God anthropomorphically, in human images, the Apter Rav
once wrote, and then asked, Does God think of us as divine
images?

Although he was not a Hasidic rebbe in the traditional sense,
my father became a rebbe in a different sense: he brought
Hasidism to the world. His writings are imbued with Hasidic
teachings, obvious to those who know Hasidic texts, and his
teachings reflect the two poles of his own attraction to Hasidism:
on the one hand, the teachings of the Baal Shem Tov, the founder
of the Hasidic movement, that emphasize love and compassion, a
tradition maintained by the Apter Rav, Levi Yitzhak of Berdichev,
and others among my father's ancestors. They were gentle and
kind, seeking to ease the sadness and anxieties of their followers
and show them the sheer joy of being a Jew. On the other hand,
there was the sharp and critical voice of the Kotzker rebbe, who
left no texts but many oral teachings demanding truth, honesty,
sincerity, and integrity, and who retreated into isolation after
being disgusted with the failings of his fellow human beings. My
father had both traditions wrestling in his soul, as he tells us in
his last book, *A Passion for Truth*. He was tender and empathic,
wanting Jews to experience Judaism as a celebration, but he was
also sharp and critical of the mendacity of the government, the
small-mindedness of religious people, and the failure of Jews to
understand their own religion. He was a critic and a comforter,
never satisfied with how things were, yet always optimistic about
the future.

Hasidic teachings and a Hasidic spirit infuse my father's writings as they did his life and his personality. So many people admire my father and draw inspiration from his writings and from his life. They strive to understand his work, and when they read his books, they think: he is speaking to me, he understands me. Indeed, what marks my father's work is the quiet intimacy he creates with his readers, which reflects the intimacy of his piety expressed in his writings on God and prayer and the Sabbath. That intimacy is so profound that he sometimes speaks allusively, as we all do when we enter the inner sanctum of the intimate.

Intimacy was part of his religious heritage; he often followed the Hasidic tradition of praying in seclusion, and when I watched him pray I could see he was in a private world. But that sense of intimacy was also present in social gatherings and at family celebrations. He brought intimacy to his closest friends and family, who confided in him, and he knew how to make his students and visitors feel special with his attentiveness and concern, which were genuine. Indeed, intimacy is a theme of his Yiddish poetry, poems that he wrote as a young man in Vilna, where he briefly studied at a Gymnasium (high school) in the 1920s.

Germany 1927–38

The inner, spiritual world of Eastern European piety is what he mourned after the war, describing it eloquently in his book *The Earth Is the Lord's,* and it is also Hasidic thought that he brought with him to Berlin when he decided to pursue a life of scholarship and enter the university. He came to Berlin in 1927, convinced that it was the intellectual center of the universe, and entered both the Reform rabbinical school and the University of Berlin, while also studying at the Hildesheimer Orthodox rabbinical seminary — probably the only student at home in all three environments. He was always eager to learn new approaches and methods, and he felt comfortable in all

Jewish settings, even as he was also critical of all of them, as he was of the academic world as well. Indeed, he often remarked that while he came to Berlin to study modern philosophical methods of analyzing religion, he felt his professors could understand religion better if they were exposed to the piety of Hasidic Judaism.

As a student in Berlin, he was alone, without family, and very poor. But he loved to study, and he worked hard. When the Great Depression struck in late 1929, he subsisted on potatoes; that was all he could afford to eat. He prayed with the Orthodox community, especially at the small synagogue of Rabbi Yehiel Weinberg, who became a close friend, and whenever possible, he traveled to Vienna to visit the growing number of relatives who had moved there, including his two married sisters, Sarah and Devorah.

While in Berlin, my father learned historical-critical methods of analyzing the Bible and rabbinic texts and took courses in philosophy and art history. He went to the theater and concerts, attended lectures, and even joined a Stefan George reading group. He studied the world of Jewish historical scholarship that had emerged in Germany during the nineteenth century. He read German philosophy thoroughly and deeply, and immersed himself in German literature and poetry. Still, he was never fully at home: he was conscious of the Germans' failure to appreciate the Hebrew Bible and Judaism, and he was dissatisfied with the narrowness of Jewish scholarly methods. Jewish scholarship focused on superficialities, he felt, and failed to appreciate the religious and poetic power of biblical and rabbinic texts. He used to shake his head when describing a professor of Bible who told his class that the repetition in Isaiah, "Comfort ye, comfort ye my people," must have been a scribal error and then struck out the second "comfort ye."

Although his doctoral dissertation, a study of the biblical prophets, *Das prophetische Bewusstsein,* was completed in late 1932, according to university regulations, he could not officially receive the Ph.D. until it was published. And yet, after Hitler came to power in January 1933 it was nearly impossible to find a publisher for a Jewish-authored book. Finally, in 1935, the book was published in Poland, and he convinced the dean to accept the publication and grant the degree, three years after he wrote it. Tragically, there was little of the prophetic consciousness that he described in his dissertation that could be found among many Germans in those days.

Hitler's rise to power was a shock, and like most German Jews my father was certain the Nazi regime would quickly collapse. The book burning outside the University of Berlin in May 1933, the forced expulsion of Jewish professors, and the silence or collaboration of many Christians, including clergy, horrified him, and, like so many others, he tried to escape. Once his dissertation was published, he tried desperately to find a teaching position outside Nazi Germany. Meanwhile, his academic work shifted and he wrote several technical articles on medieval Jewish philosophy, as well as a popular biography of Maimonides, whose eight hundredth birthday was being celebrated in 1935.

My father's work was not only academic; he was invited to lecture to various Jewish communities in Germany that were feeling the isolation imposed by the Nazi Reich. He spoke to them about Jewish thinkers, such as Abravanel, who noted that Spain's expulsion of the Jews in 1492 meant they did not become participants in the bloody Spanish conquests that followed. And he also scolded German Jews for being inverted Marranos (Jewish on the outside, Christian on the inside) and urged them to recover their Jewish heritage. This meant, as he told Martin Buber over tea one afternoon in 1936, not simply instructing Jewish adults in the words of the prayerbook, but conveying to them what it means to pray.

When Buber left for Palestine in 1937, he invited my father to replace him at the adult Jewish education center in Frankfurt am Main, which he had established with Franz Rosenzweig. There my father taught until his arrest in October 1938 and deportation to Poland. He had already received an invitation to move to the United States and teach at the Hebrew Union College, the Reform rabbinical college in Cincinnati, but he had not yet received a visa from the American consulate. Finally, in the summer of 1939, just weeks before the Nazi invasion, he left Warsaw for England, where he thought, correctly, that it might be easier to obtain the American visa. He stayed there with his brother Jacob and his family before departing by ship for the United States in March of 1940.

Had Hitler not come to power, my father's life would no doubt have followed the course taken by other talented Jewish scholars of the era: he would have completed his doctorate and his Habilitation (second degree), and received a teaching position at a rabbinical college or a German university — assuming the Germans would have overcome their prejudice against Jewish studies and established professorships at their universities. He would have married, fathered children, and become a scholar and a leading voice in the European Jewish community and in the Jewish-Christian dialogue that was just beginning to emerge before the Nazis destroyed everything.

Life in the United States

My father almost never spoke of leaving his mother and three of his sisters behind in Europe. When he did, he broke down completely. One sister, Esther, was killed during the first weeks of the Nazi invasion of Poland in September 1939; his mother and his sister Gittel remained in Warsaw and were able to send him postcards until the fall of 1942, when they, too, were murdered. He remained hopeful that his sister Devorah, who had been living in Vienna with her husband, had survived, and he tried after the war to locate her, via the Red Cross, only to learn that she had been deported to Teresienstadt in 1942 and then to Auschwitz in 1944, where she was murdered on arrival; her husband was killed in the Riga ghetto. So many friends and family were killed — "almost everyone who knew me as a child," he used to say; his world was wiped out. And he never returned to Poland, Germany, or Austria.

My father's five years in Cincinnati were difficult. He lived in a dormitory room at the Hebrew Union College, where he kept a small refrigerator because the college cafeteria was not kosher at that time. He had no family or close friends in the area, and he was still learning English and trying to adjust to teaching American students, who had very little Hebrew preparation for their studies. He tried desperately to save his mother and three sisters. Whenever possible, he traveled to New York to be with his sister, Sarah, and her husband, the Kopitzinitzer rebbe, who lived on the Lower East Side, and with his cousins, the Novominsker rebbe and the Boyaner rebbe.

Just before leaving Cincinnati and moving to New York, where he became a professor at the Jewish Theological Seminary, my father met my mother, Sylvia Straus, who was studying piano with Severin Eisenberger. She, too, moved to New York, to study with another pianist, Eduard Steuermann, and soon my parents were engaged and married, in December of 1946.

I am still amazed by my father's courage, after losing his family in the war, to fall in love, marry, and have a child. I must add: he was never depressed, never moody or withdrawn or melancholy. Our family home was filled with laughter, jokes, playfulness. He knew how to celebrate: my parents would share a box of special crackers and a bottle of beer to mark a special occasion. We would buy a cupcake and light a birthday candle on top to celebrate the publication of his latest book. All it took was the right spirit, and he could transform mundane crackers into a gourmet experience. My mother, a pianist, spent her days practicing and caring for the household. In the evenings, after dinner, my father would either return to his office at the Seminary or retreat to his study at home, but first he would sit in his favorite chair in the living room and ask my mother to play for him — Bach or Mozart or Brahms or Chopin. One evening a week, we had chamber music — piano trios or quartets — followed by tea and cake and conversation, which my father would join. On other evenings, after reading and writing that followed dinner, my parents would have a cup of tea and talk, sometimes playing rounds of Chinese checkers, which my father invariably won.

During the first years of their marriage, before I was born, my father suddenly became intensely productive. He had arrived in the United States barely able to speak English, but after five years in Cincinnati, his English was fluent and magnificent, although he also continued to write in Hebrew and Yiddish. In the first six years of his marriage, he published *The Earth Is the Lord's*; *The Sabbath*; *Man Is Not Alone*; *God In Search of Man*; and *Man's Quest for God,* a remarkable achievement. *The Earth is the Lord's* was first presented, in shortened form, as a lecture in Yiddish that my father delivered to members of YIVO, the Yiddish Scientific Research Center in New York. It was a panegyric to the lost Hasidic spiritual world of Eastern Europe, and although the YIVO members were staunchly secular, the speech was so moving that they spontaneously arose at the end and together recited Kaddish, the prayer of mourning. His book *The Sabbath* followed, as a kind of comfort for the loss: "The Sabbath comes like a caress, wiping away fear, sorrow and somber memories."

In trying to reintroduce the importance of the Sabbath to American Jews who were assimilating and assuming that religion would soon be a relic of the past, my father did not berate Jews for their neglect of religious observance, nor did he demand obedience to Jewish law based on the absolute authority of rabbinic texts. Writing in an era in which books by clergy advocating the psychological health promoted by religion were coming into vogue, my father went against the trend. He insisted that the Sabbath is not about psychology or sociology; it doesn't serve to make us calmer or to hold the family together. Nor does the Sabbath represent a rejection of modernity or the secular world. For him, the Sabbath was a complement to building civilization, not a withdrawal from it. In contrast to more recent approaches to the Sabbath, my father did not emphasize the importance of "ritual" (he believed that the words "customs and ceremonies" should be eradicated from the Jewish vocabulary), nor did he view the Sabbath as a vehicle for solidifying Jewish continuity.

Rather, he writes that we need the Sabbath in order to survive civilization: "Gallantly, ceaselessly, quietly, we must fight for inner liberty," to remain independent of the enslavement of the material world. How do we bring about the elusive atmosphere that is the Sabbath? Sanctity is a quality, my father emphasized, that we create. We know what to do with space, but how do we shape sacred time? Six days a week we embezzle our lives with a fury of acquisitiveness, he writes; Shabbat renews the soul and we rediscover who we are. "The Sabbath is the presence of God in the world, open to the soul of man." It was on the seventh day that God gave the world a soul and "the world's survival depends upon the holiness of the seventh day." The task, he writes, becomes how to convert time into eternity, how to fill our time with spirit.

How are we to make the Sabbath holy? How do we perceive the presence of God in the world? These are the questions that open my father's books published in the postwar years. In *Man Is Not Alone* and *God in Search of Man* he does not try to prove the existence of God, but asks how we human beings can cultivate our inner lives to become aware that it is God who is searching for us. Experiences of wonder, awe, and radical amazement can lead us to a deeper perception of being the object of divine concern and being able to respond to God's need for us, God's challenge to us to repair the universe.

These books appeared at a time when assimilating American Jews were embarrassed by public expressions of Jewishness. Even among rabbis and Jewish leaders a rejection of Jewish mysticism, Hasidism, and even of theology and spirituality was common. It was as if they desired a religionless Judaism — a Judaism without God, faith, or belief, simply for ethnicity and community. For them, the Sabbath interfered with jobs, socializing, shopping, and simply being American. His work

was not immediately understood, especially by his seminary colleagues, who were often contemptuous of his interests. He felt
isolated, disappointed, and at times insecure. Much of what he
viewed as the heart of Judaism — Hasidism, Kabbalah, rabbinic theology — the seminary faculty considered irrelevant or
even nonsense. Rather than teaching advanced seminars to rabbinical students, he was assigned to give introductory courses
to the teacher's institute. He had no one to talk to and felt
terribly lonely. A turning point was a glorious review of his
book *Man Is Not Alone,* written by Reinhold Niebuhr for the
New York Herald Tribune. The Sunday that it appeared my
parents expected their friends and colleagues to phone and con-
gratulate my father; the phone didn't ring all day. That was
just one example they used to give me of the jealousy and
mean-spiritedness of academic life.

Relations with Christians

My father was deeply moved by his friendship with Niebuhr
and used to say that Niebuhr understood his work better than
anyone else; finally he had someone to talk to, someone who
understood theology. Imagine what it meant for my father to
flee from Nazi Germany, where some distinguished Protestant
theologians were calling for the elimination of the Old Testament from the Christian Bible because a Jewish book had no
place in a Nazi society, while others, Protestant and Catholic,
defended the Old Testament on the grounds that it was not a
Jewish book, but an anti-Jewish book: the prophets constantly
denounced Israel for its sins. Then he came to the United States
and met Niebuhr, who deeply appreciated the Hebrew Bible,
and soon became close to a diverse range of Christian pas-
tors and theologians, including John C. Bennett, William Sloane
Coffin, Martin Luther King, W. D. Davies, Bayard Rustin,
James Sanders, Andrew Young, Dorothy Day, Sister Mary
Corita, Daniel Day Williams, Jesse Jackson, James Muilenburg,

Roger Shinn, Gustave Weigel, Richard John Neuhaus, Abbot Leo Rudloff, and many others.

My father's approach to Christians was unique and distinctive among modern Jewish theologians. The modern era opened with Moses Mendelssohn's cordial relationships with Christians and their avoidance of direct discussions of theological differences. Abraham Geiger, a pioneering theologian of the nineteenth century, threw down a gauntlet to Christians (especially Protestants on the quest for the historical figure of Jesus) when he claimed that Jesus was a Jew who said nothing new or original, but followed the path of the liberalizing Pharisees. The faith of Jesus was Judaism, Geiger insisted; Christianity was the religion about him, devised by Paul who polluted Jewish monotheism with pagan ideas to create Christian doctrine. Early twentieth-century Jewish thinkers were either disdainful of Christianity (Hermann Cohen), granted Christianity a role in spreading Jewish ideas that will ultimately lead to redemption (Franz Rosenzweig), or viewed Jesus as a brother (Martin Buber).

My father's approach was entirely different. Almost never did he mention Jesus or Paul, or engage in exegesis of New Testament texts. He rarely discussed, in public, the history of Christian anti-Semitism, including the role of the churches and the Vatican during the Holocaust. He was never patronizing toward Christian scholars of Jewish texts, but he did have intense discussions of rabbinic ideas with them. What he expected from Christians is precisely what he displayed: respect, affirmation, public support, and never an attempt at conversion, which he considered existential violence. When invited to speak to Christian groups, at colleges, or meetings of clergy, he most often spoke about God, prayer, and the nature of human life, making the same points he did to Jewish groups. He sought topics that unite us rather than divide us.

For a Jew from the Hasidic world to have close personal relationships with Christian theologians is remarkable. What did they talk about? The bond was always the Bible and how to understand it. But there were other topics: he discussed rabbinic texts with W. D. Davies, a scholar of Pauline theology; with James Sanders, scholar of the Bible and Dead Sea Scrolls, he would discuss the prophets and related rabbinic passages. Many of those Christian friends joined our family for the Passover Seder or for a Shabbat dinner; indeed, my father invited Martin Luther King Jr. and his family to join us for the Passover Seder in that fateful year of 1968; Dr. King was assassinated just days before Passover. Sometimes his Christian colleagues came to him for advice: a community of nuns asked if he thought they should abandon their traditional habit; Bill Coffin grieved over his divorce.

They collaborated on efforts to end the war in Vietnam, to understand the meaning of Zionism and the State of Israel, and to conquer poverty. Martin Luther King joined him in speaking out for the release of Jews from the Soviet Union, Abbott Leo Rudloff, of the Weston Priory in Vermont, was an avid public defender of Israel's security, and my father joined Jesse Jackson in Operation Breadbasket.

In most cases, Christians sought out his friendship, eager to better understand his reading of the Bible, and to gain insight into the nature of prayer, but often it was his person, as a religious Jew, that attracted them: theirs was a dialogue of depth-theology, an encounter of one religious person with another, as he describes in his writings. The purpose, he said in his inaugural lecture as the Harry Emerson Fosdick Visiting Professor at Union Theological Seminary in 1964, was not to discuss what divides Jews and Christians — the divinity of Jesus, for example — but "to help one another; to share insight and learning, to cooperate in academic ventures on the highest scholarly level and, what is even more important, to search in the wilderness for wellsprings of devotion, for treasures of stillness... helping one another in the terrible predicament of here and now by the courage to believe that the word of the Lord endures forever as well as in the here and now."

His encounters with Pope Paul VI, Cardinal Augustin Bea, and other leading Catholics during the Second Vatican Council were meetings of the spirit. Their conversations centered on what Jews and Christians share: the Hebrew Bible, experiences of prayer, belief in God's presence in their lives. While some Jews criticized my father for his ecumenical work, he believed it was a sacred task. When he arrived for a private audience in March 1971, Pope Paul VI, my father wrote in his diary, "smiled joyously, with a radiant face, shook my hand cordially with both hands...telling me that he is reading my books, that my books are very spiritual and very beautiful, and that Catholics should read my books." Toward the end of the meeting, my father writes, "I told him how grateful we Jews are for the understanding he has shown for the spiritual link of the Jewish people with the Holy City of Jerusalem. All of Jewish history is a pilgrimage to Jerusalem, and the union of the Jewish people and the city of Jerusalem we regard as a sign of divine grace and providence in this age of darkness. The pope then said: 'I will remember your words' and added: 'I hope that you and I will meet together in Jerusalem.' I then said he may feel assured that the Jews of Israel will treat the holy places of Christianity with deep reverence. He then said: 'God bless you.' I said 'God bless you.'"

My father's involvement with the Vatican had begun during the Second Vatican Council, conceived by Pope John XXIII. He was asked by the American Jewish Committee (AJC) in 1962 to help draft a memorandum that would alter the tone of discussions concerning Catholic-Jewish relations and he wrote:

With humility and in the spirit of commitment to the prophets of Israel, let us consider the grave problems that confront us all as the children of God. Both Judaism and Christianity share the prophets' belief that God chooses agents through whom His will is made known and His work done throughout history. Both Judaism and Christianity live in the certainty that mankind is in need of ultimate redemption, that God is involved in human history, that in relations between man and man, God is at stake.

My father held meetings with various Vatican representatives, both in New York and in Rome, although he was frequently attacked in bitter terms by some of his Jewish colleagues who felt that theological dialogue with Christians was forbidden to Jews and that Jews were demeaning themselves by negotiating with the church over *Nostra Aetate* (Vatican II's historic Declaration on the Relation between the Church and Non-Christian Religions). But my father felt that the lives of Jews were at stake in Christian teachings about Judaism. He had lived through too much not to be aware of the power of language. He used to point out that Hitler had come to power not with tanks and machine guns, but with words, and he always emphasized the importance of guarding one's tongue. In his memorandum for the AJC, he wrote:

> It is from the inner life of men and from the articulation of evil thoughts that evil actions take their rise. It is therefore of extreme importance that the sinfulness of thoughts of suspicion and hatred and particularly the sinfulness of any contemptuous utterance, however flippantly it is meant, be made clear to all mankind. This applies in particular to such thoughts and utterances about individuals or groups of other religions, races, and nations.

Most significant was the personal dimension of my father's encounters with Christians. He never reproached them; his topic was not to speak about the specific anti-Jewish prejudices of Christian theology, nor about the failures of the Vatican during the Holocaust. But he didn't need to be explicit: in his sheer being as a religious Jew, without saying a word Christians who encountered him suddenly confronted their conscience. He used to ask his Christian friends, Is it really *ad majorem Dei gloriam*, to the greater glory of God, that there should be no more

Jews in the world, that the Sabbath should come to an end, that the Torah should no longer be read in synagogues? Thus, when the Second Vatican Council proposed a draft resolution in 1964 calling for the eventual conversion of the Jews, my father responded, "I would rather go to Auschwitz than give up my faith." The final declaration, *Nostra Aetate* (1965), affirmed the continuing covenant between Jews and God and clarified that not all Jews are responsible for the crucifixion. Further, it deplored anti-Semitism and did not call for the Jews' conversion, a remarkable turning point that Rabbi Gilbert Rosenthal called "a Copernican revolution in Catholic thinking about the Jewish religion and people."[2]

The declaration was the result of intellectual changes, to be sure, but also of personal encounters between Catholics and Jews. It was a surprising experience for Christians in those days to discover they could learn something about God from a Jew, that the theology of a Jew could make them better Christians. Many thought that had not happened for two thousand years, since Jesus and Paul. Experiencing the Sabbath in our home, listening as my father prayed, they found themselves brought to a deeper level of their own spiritual lives. Watching as a child, it seemed to me that the nuns who came to our home for a visit were on a pilgrimage, coming home to the Judaism that was the womb of their own faith. This was the first Shabbat dinner or Passover Seder for many of the Christian religious who visited us, though some quickly became regular guests. Some of the nuns in their habits were tentative at first, but quickly responded to my father's gentle humor; other visitors, especially Father Felix Morlion from Rome, regaled us with jokes and theological banter. "My friend," my father would say, putting his hand on Bill Coffin's arm, "Would you like to learn the prayer for bread, the *hamotzi?*" And then he would teach Bill the Hebrew words. Discussions of theology would lead him to

---

2. Gilbert S. Rosenthal, *What Can a Modern Jew Believe?* (Eugene, Ore.: Wipf and Stock, 2007), 210.

tell a story, sometimes from the Midrash, often about one of his Hasidic ancestors.

What was clear to me was the revelation these devout Christians were experiencing: Judaism, they discovered, was not about legalism or outdated rituals, but spiritual vitality. Were those who rejected Christ to be denied salvation, as the church had long claimed? Suddenly they realized that my father, too, would of course be welcomed into heaven — and please recognize what a profound theological earthquake that represented for so many Christians in that era.

For my father, the personal friendships with Christians were deeply moving. He was able to speak freely about theology and spirituality in a discussion that had not yet taken shape in the Jewish community in America; many American Jews were still insisting, anachronistically, that Judaism has no theology. But imagine: as a child my father had crossed the street rather than walk in front of a church, and now he found himself consulted by Christians about liturgical reform, social justice, and biblical interpretation, as well as meeting with the pope and Vatican officials to overcome centuries of Christian efforts to convert Jews and blame them for the death of Jesus. For my father, such encounters were momentous. He considered it an upheaval in the history of the West and a God-given mandate for his work.

The Political as Spiritual

Although his life was saved by the Reform movement's Hebrew Union College and he taught for most of his career at the Conservative movement's Jewish Theological Seminary, my father never identified with any of the movements, and he freely criticized all of them: they were insufficiently attentive to Jewish law or too strict in the wrong areas of religious observance. As an epigraph to his Hebrew study of rabbinic theology, my father wrote, "Small-mindedness brings the exile of the Torah." And that was what he often encountered. He once asked his rabbinical students, "Is gelatin kosher?" which sparked a lively discussion, but when he then asked "Are nuclear weapons kosher?" the students were silent; they didn't know how to begin to answer. Synagogues, my father complained, were too big and alienating; he said that American Jews suffered from an edifice complex; Jews had become messengers who had forgotten the message; the congregation was sitting back and letting the rabbi and cantor pray for them, vicariously. God was in exile in those congregations, replaced by "customs and ceremonies." My father's spiritual home was the world of prayer, and wherever he was, he stopped for the afternoon prayers — even on a busy street corner on Fifth Avenue. His spiritual rejuvenation came when he had the opportunity to pray on a Sabbath or holiday at a Hasidic shtiebl (a small, intimate prayer room).

Political issues were moral issues, religious imperatives — that was the message I received constantly at home. Vietnam was a grave moral issue, as was the racism in American society, which horrified my father. In 1963, after speaking at a conference on "Religion and Race" (two words, he said, that should never be uttered in the same breath), he met Martin Luther King Jr. and formed an extraordinary friendship. The bond my father felt with Dr. King was religious, and what linked them was the Bible, especially the prophets. Theirs was a relationship on the level of what my father called "depth theology," the fear and trembling in the hearts of pious people, regardless of their religion. My father said he was reminded at the 1965 Voting Rights march in Selma, Alabama, of what it had been like walking with Hasidic rebbes in Europe; he felt a sense of holiness in the Selma march. He brought to Selma, as he did to all demonstrations, his religious commitment and only regretted, he said, that Jewish organizations had not conveyed to the young people who had taken part that the civil rights movement bore a Jewish religious significance in terms of prophetic teachings. At Selma, he said, "I felt my legs were praying."

The organization my father co-founded to protest the war in Vietnam, Clergy and Laymen Concerned about Vietnam, became the forum for Martin Luther King to speak out against the war, which he did at a gathering of two thousand people at Riverside Church, in New York City, on April 4, 1967, exactly one year to the day before he was assassinated. My father had worried for some time about whether Dr. King should speak out against the war; how would such a sharp criticism of U.S. policy affect the support of Congress and the president for the civil rights movement? Lacking widespread support even within the SCLC for a public position against the war, King came under severe attack for his opposition. Major newspapers within both the black and white communities editorialized against him, and civil rights leaders including Ralph Bunche, Whitney Young, Roy Wilkins, Jackie Robinson, and Senator Edward Brooke publicly criticized him.[3] SNCC and CORE opposed the war, but the larger, more powerful and mainstream organizations, including the NAACP, defended it. Whitney Young, president of the National Urban League, also opposed King, stating, "the greatest freedom that exists for Negroes... is the freedom to die in Vietnam."[4]

When Dr. King stood at the podium at Riverside Church, he spoke with extraordinary courage and delivered one of the great speeches of his life. "If America's soul becomes totally poisoned, part of the autopsy must read Vietnam.... The world now demands a maturity of America that we may not be able to achieve. It demands that we admit that we have been wrong from the beginning of our adventure in Vietnam, that we have been detrimental to the life of the Vietnamese people.... In order to atone for our sins and errors in Vietnam, we should take the initiative in bringing a halt to this tragic war."

---

3. Frederick J. Antczak, "When 'Silence Is Betrayal': An Ethical Criticism of the Revolution of Values in the Speech at Riverside Church," in *Martin Luther King, Jr., and the Sermonic Power of Public Discourse*, ed. Carolyn Calloway-Thomas and John Louis Lucaites (Tuscaloosa: University of Alabama Press, 1993), 134–35.

4. Adam Fairclough, "The Southern Christian Leadership Conference and the Second Reconstruction, 1957–1973," *Southern Atlantic Quarterly* 80, no. 2 (Spring 1981): 177–94; reprinted in *Native American Religion and Black Protestantism*, ed. Martin E. Marty (Munich: K. G. Sauer, 1993): 188–205.

My father, who lectured frequently at antiwar rallies, made his opposition to the war an integral part of his public lectures and his classes. He invited Daniel Berrigan to his seminar on Hasidic texts to discuss the war and the debate about how to respond: Dan and his brother, Phil Berrigan, chose civil disobedience and prison as an act of symbolic protest, but my father felt he could be more effective out of prison, speaking out against the war. He vigorously condemned the atrocities committed by U.S. forces in Vietnam and the obvious political futility of a war against guerillas, and he was placed under FBI surveillance and branded an anti-American subversive by supporters of the war. He was also attacked by members of the Jewish community, who feared his public opposition to the war would undermine American support for the State of Israel. But the real subversiveness, my father stated in his introduction of Martin Luther King Jr. at Riverside Church in 1967, came from the policies of the American government:

> It is our duty as citizens to say no to the subversiveness of our government, which is ruining the values we cherish.... If mercy, the mother of humility, is still alive as a demand, how can we say yes to our bringing agony to a tormented country? We are here because our own integrity as human beings is decaying in the agony and merciless killing done in our name. In a free society, some are guilty and all are responsible.... Remember that blood of the innocent cries forever. Should that blood stop to cry, humanity would cease to be.

The crimes committed in Vietnam were destroying American values, and were also undermining our religious lives, he insisted. Someone may commit a crime now and teach mathematics an hour later, but when we pray, all we have done in our lives enters our prayers.[5] As he had articulated in his early

---

5. Abraham Heschel, "The Holy Dimension," in *Moral Grandeur and Spiritual Audacity: Essays by Abraham Joshua Heschel,* ed. Susannah Heschel (New York: Farrar, Straus & Giroux, 1996), 318–27.

essays of the 1940s, the purpose of prayer is not petitionary. We do not pray in order to be saved, my father stressed in his writings; we pray so that we might be worthy of being saved. Prayer should not focus on our wishes, but rather is a moment in which God's intentions are reflected in us.[6] If we are created in the image of God, each human being should be a reminder of God's presence. If we engage in acts of violence and murder, we are desecrating the divine likeness.

Both my father and Dr. King spoke of each other as prophets. On March 25, 1968, just ten days before he was assassinated, Dr. King delivered the keynote address at a birthday celebration honoring my father, convened by the Rabbinical Assembly of America, an umbrella organization of Conservative rabbis. In his introduction of Dr. King to the audience, my father asked, "Where in America today do we hear a voice like the voice of the prophets of Israel? Martin Luther King is a sign that God has not forsaken the United States of America. God has sent him to us. His presence is the hope of America. His mission is sacred, his leadership of supreme importance to every one of us." In his address, King stated that my father "is indeed a truly great prophet." He went on, "Here and there we find those who refuse to remain silent behind the safe security of stained-glass windows, and they are forever seeking to make the great ethical insights of our Judeo-Christian heritage relevant in this day and in this age. I feel that Rabbi Heschel is one of the persons who is relevant at all times, always standing with prophetic insights to guide us through these difficult days."[7]

It is clear that their relationship carried profound meaning for both my father and Dr. King. They seem to have been aware of the symbolic significance of their friendship and used it as a tool to foster further alliances between Jews and blacks. My father worked on joint projects with Jesse Jackson and Wyatt T. Walker, among others, while many of King's closest advisors

---

6. Heschel, "Prayer," in ibid., 340–53.
7. The texts of both speeches are reprinted in ibid., 657–79.

were Jews. The opposition of most Jewish organizations to affirmative action programs, beginning in the 1970s, never won support from my father, who died in 1972, and it is likely he would have mediated the tensions arising from the Jewish community's hostility toward Andrew Young and Jesse Jackson that developed in the late 1970s and 1980s. Yet while my father gave his political support to a wide range of African-American leaders, it was the spiritual affinity he experienced with King that lent their relationship a particularly strong and profound intimacy.

Religion as Challenge and Embarrassment

Unlike his contemporaries in the era of 1950s and 1960s America, my father did not see religion as a tool to calm fears, alleviate social stress, and keep the family together. Religion may comfort the afflicted, he said, but it also must afflict the comfortable. In a series of lectures he delivered at Stanford University in 1963, published as *Who Is Man?* in 1965, he argued that religion is a challenge that begins with a sense of embarrassment. God, he stated, "is not only a power we depend on; He is a God who demands."[8] My father grounded his understanding of religion not only in Scripture, but also in the complexity of human life: what it is to be a human being and how to create a sense of authenticity. The depth of religious life required a depth of self-exploration and understanding.

The human being was always at the forefront of his thought: for example, he responded to the Holocaust not by discussing the problem of evil as an abstract force, but the problem of human suffering and its expression in religion. Yet he did not stop with human experience, but pointed out that human suffering was understood in rabbinic thought as a moment to identify with God's suffering and also a challenge to overcome evils, one by one, through justice. The Holocaust, for him, was not

---

8. Heschel, *Who Is Man?* (Stanford: Stanford University Press, 1965), 109.

an issue of theodicy, but of anthropodicy: how could God keep faith in us after the atrocities we have committed?

Religion comes not to explain, but to express and to challenge. As Karl Marx wrote, "Religious suffering is at the same time an expression of real suffering and a protest against real suffering. Religion is the sigh of the oppressed creature, the heart of a heartless world, and the soul of soulless conditions. It is the opium of the people."[9] Marx's language has an echo in my father's study of the prophets when he writes, "The prophet's ear perceives the silent sigh" of human anguish. Religion is not merely experience, but action; justice, my father asserts, is the tool of God, the manifestation of God, the means of our redemption and the redemption of God from human mendacity.

Religion, he writes, "begins with the certainty that something is asked of us, that there are ends which are in need of us."[10] Religion does not come to provide us with assurance, nor is it about generating guilt or shame. Religion rather evokes obligation, our response to "ends that are in need of us."[11] Religion may begin with a sense of mystery, awe, wonder, and fear, but religion itself is concerned with "what to do with the feeling for the mystery of living, what to do with awe, wonder, or fear."[12] Other theologians of the day omitted the sense of obligation that derived from theology. By contrast, religion for my father had to pick up the challenge articulated by Marx: "The philosophers have only interpreted the world in various ways; the point however is to change it."[13] Religion was not mere

9. *Karl Marx: Early Writings,* trans. T. B. Bottomore (London: C. A. Watts 1963), 43–44; cited by Alistair Kee, *Marx and the Failure of Liberation Theology* (London: SCM Press, 1990), 32–33.

10. Abraham Joshua Heschel, *Man Is Not Alone: A Philosophy of Religion* (New York: Farrar, Straus and Young, 1951), 215.

11. Ibid.

12. Abraham Joshua Heschel, *God in Search of Man* (New York: Farrar, Straus and Cudahy, 1955), 162

13. Karl Marx and Frederick Engels, *Collected Works* (London: Lawrence & Wishart, 1973–); cited by Alistair Kee, *The Rise and Demise of Black Theology* (Aldershot, England: Ashgate, 2006), 214.

subjectivity, for my father, but has to lead to action: "What gives birth to religion is not intellectual curiosity but the fact and experience of our being asked."[14] What is human existence? My father says: "*I am commanded — therefore I am.*"[15] Human consciousness has built into it a sense of indebtedness. Those are the moments he identifies as "prophetic moments."

Religious Observance

Always observant, my father was nonetheless insistent that we cannot live as Jews today the way we lived yesterday. Change is imperative. Like Pope John XXIII, whom he quoted, he realized that no edifice, no religion can survive without repair from time to time. Only God is perfect, and the great fault with Jews today, he said, is that we have confused God with *halakha* (Jewish law). We have lost sight of God, substituting *halakha* as immutable, omnipotent, and omniscient; he called that religious behaviorism. We worry about the future of the Jewish people and have lost sight of the needs of the individual Jew, he wrote, and while we have focused tremendous attention on the political problem of the Jewish people as a collective, we have neglected our inner, private, spiritual lives. Sermons, he said, have become platitudes, failing to recognize the anguish in so many people's lives. Enough with demographics and community surveys, he insisted; spend the money on education, on teachers' salaries. What we need are not textbooks, but text people: teachers whose own lives exemplify what it means to be a Jew and inspire their pupils. Such scolding did not endear him to Jewish leaders or to rabbis; he was frequently attacked and denounced. My mother would comfort him, but also beg him at times to tone down his comments. Yet he always said

---

14. Heschel, *God in Search of Man*, 112.
15. Heschel, *Who Is Man?* 111.

he felt it was his duty to tell his audience what they needed to hear, not what they wanted to hear.

Our religious lives at home were Orthodox. Some Jews speak of being "strictly observant"; I think my father was lovingly observant. We kept kosher, observed the Sabbath and holidays, and attended synagogue services at the Jewish Theological Seminary where my father taught. My parents led quiet lives: my father read, my mother played the piano, and only on rare occasion did they attend a theater or concert — almost never a movie. On Sabbath afternoons, they invited students to tea, and occasionally there were guests for Friday night Shabbat dinners. That, too, gave me a sense of family intimacy — just the three of us (I am an only child) talking, reading, laughing. My father loved to play a game of speaking only the first half of a sentence, to see if my mother or I could finish it for him — and we always did. When we had guests, most of whom were European refugee scholars, dinner conversations were about German culture and intellectual life or about Hasidic rebbes and their teachings. Although raised in a very traditional, gender-differentiated pietistic home, my father recognized that aspects of Judaism had to change, particularly for women. He asked me to lead prayers at the table, and he even suggested that I consider becoming a Conservative rabbi, at a time when women's ordination seemed highly remote. I was the first daughter of my parents' circle to have a Bat Mitzvah celebration at a synagogue on Shabbat morning, at my request, and my parents were fully supportive. My father used to say that while he was expected to become a Hasidic rebbe, he felt the world needed something different from him — and Jewish women needed more as well.

My father's last books were written in the midst of the escalating war in Vietnam, a war that made him sick, and his shock at the mendacity of American politicians and the callousness of a government killing thousands of innocent civilians was one reason he wrote *Kotzk,* his two-volume Yiddish study of the nineteenth-century Hasidic rebbe, Menachem Mendel of

Kotzk.[16] It was a book that examined the Kotzker's outrage over mendacity, and at a certain point my father's speeches against the war and the teachings of the Kotzker begin to merge. There is a will to be deceived, both said; like the Kotzker, my father warned against deception and imitation, including the imitation of oneself. Even as the lies of politicians were abhorrent, so was the gullibility of Americans.

Don't deceive and don't imitate, the Kotzker insisted. Not to deceive means not to deceive oneself, but also not to imitate oneself. The Kotzer denounced pious Jews for trying with all their strength to preserve tradition; even customs become holy if they're old. They look askance at any new practices and view Orthodox Jews as the only authentic Jews. "Innovation is forbidden by the Torah" is a major rule — but the Kotzker ethos holds that Jewishness must be new. Prayer must be as fresh as a new insight in interpretation, and thought must be quivering with novelty. Repetition and imitation are forbidden. Just as a pair of someone else's shoes won't fit your feet, so too you can't serve God with someone else's ideas. Religion must continually evolve, in practice and interpretation: "A vibrant society does not dwell in the shadows of old ideas and viewpoints; in the realm of the spirit, only a pioneer can be a true heir. The wages of spiritual plagiarism are the loss of integrity; self-aggrandizement is self-betrayal. Authentic faith is more than an echo of a tradition. It is a creative situation, an event."[17] That approach is far from the teachings of Reform and Conservative rabbis, who, my father felt, had abandoned *halakha* in trying to make Judaism comfortable and compatible with suburban lifestyles.

One may not imitate others and one may not imitate oneself, the Kotzker taught. Imitation is false. Therefore one is forbidden to be old. And the problem is that people grow old while still young. The Kotzker claimed that freshness stands higher

---

16. Abraham Joshua Heschel, *Kotzk: The Struggle for Integrity* (Tel Aviv: Hamenora, 1973).

17. Heschel, *Man Is Not Alone*, 164.

than piety. Here is my father: Small-mindedness brings the exile
of the Torah, and literal-mindedness is an obstacle to faith.
Literal readings of Scripture and rigid adherence to religious
practice led to what he decried as "religious behaviorism."
Authenticity is not to live Judaism as our grandparents did. My
father did not prescribe a particular Jewish path but acknowledged that there are many ways of being Jewish; authenticity
is too personal for Judaism to be prescribed collectively. "Religion is an answer to man's ultimate questions," my father writes
on the first page of *God in Search of Man;* the problem is that
we human beings have forgotten the question (*GSM,* 168–69).
Similarly, we think we are in search of an elusive God, not realizing that it is God who is in search of us. How do we recover
the questions and how do we retrieve the awareness of God's
longing for us? Our lives, he writes toward the end of *A Passion for Truth,* are like chains that confine God; how do we live
lives that magnify God's presence in the world? "Religious living consists in serving ends which are in need of us. Man is not
an innocent bystander in the cosmic drama. There is in us more
kinship with the divine than we are able to believe. The souls of
men are candles of the Lord."

1

If You Want to Know God,
Sharpen Your Sense of the Human

Most philosophies of religion begin with proofs for the existence of God. My father begins with explorations of human subjectivity. He opens his earliest major works, Man Is Not Alone *(1950) and* God in Search of Man *(1951) with discussions of human experiences of awe and wonder, suggesting that an understanding of God can begin only by cultivating ourselves: What will make us receptive to God's presence?*

Religion declined, he writes on the first page of God in Search of Man, *not because of the challenges of science and philosophy, but because religion was presented in a way that was insipid. If religion is an answer to ultimate questions, we cannot realize its profundity unless we ask the right questions — but these have been forgotten. What are the right questions to be posed by theologians, scholars, and clergy? My father was continually challenging rabbis and ministers to present sermons that were integral to worship, not an intermission. Sermons should not reassure congregants, he said, but recognize the anguish in most people's lives. That, indeed, is what religion recognizes: our human agonies as well as joys.*

In 1964 my father was asked to deliver a series of five lectures at Stanford University. His chosen topic was Who Is Man?, *published as a small volume the following year. The* book begins with the assertion that human beings have very few friends left in the world. Scientists, for example, like to compare humans to animals, making it clear how much we have in common. But what is unique about being a human? The question seems to have been lost among many contemporary thinkers, leaving us uncertain what we even mean when we speak of our humanity.

"Stand still and consider the wondrous works of the Lord," says Job. Yet our sense of wonder is declining, my father writes, and with it our humanity deteriorates and also our ability to be aware of God's presence: "Awareness of the divine begins with wonder," he writes. We come to this awareness through various paths — through study of Torah and good deeds and also through nature. Nature itself sings to God, according to an old Jewish teaching, and the grandeur of nature does not encompass God, but points to God.

"The beginning of wisdom is awe of God," the Bible often states, which my father translates: Embarrassment, loss of face is the beginning of faith; it will make room within us. There is no self-assurance or complacency in a religious person; a religious person could never say, I am a good person. He writes, "I am afraid of people who are never embarrassed at their own pettiness, prejudices, envy, and conceit, never embarrassed at the profanation of life" (WIM, 114). Embarrassment is meant to be productive; the end of embarrassment would be a callousness that would mark the end of humanity.

Much of modern religious thought began with the terms of Protestant theologian Friedrich Schleiermacher, who spoke of a feeling of absolute dependence. Paul Tillich, who exerted a profound influence on American religious thought during the 1950s, held that ultimate concern generated a sense of sufficiency. My father, by contrast, saw religion originating in ultimate embarrassment, rather than dependence, inner peace, or self-esteem. What does he mean by embarrassment? In Who Is Man? he defines embarrassment as "the awareness of the incongruity of character and challenge, of perceptivity and reality, of knowledge and understanding, of mystery and comprehension" (WIM, 112). At stake ethically is not the individual act, but the cultivation of an engaged person for whom the suffering of others is intolerable and the need to respond is inescapable: "The primary problem is not how to endow particular deeds with meaning but rather how to live one's total being, how to shape one's total existence as a pattern of meaning" (WIM, 98).

The journalist Chris Hedges has written that war is a force that gives us meaning — and isn't that precisely the sort of horrific truth that constitutes the embarrassment we should feel about our human condition, as my father argues. We ought to look at the misery of human beings and realize the insufficiency of our lives; we ought to experience our own inner anguish and realize the fallacy of expediency.

Embarrassment is the foundation of religiosity and also of ethics. Yet it must not stop at that point. Embarrassment is the impulse that must lead to an awareness of being challenged. For my father the ethical is always at the forefront. Let me reconstruct some arguments he made as brief notations in the early 1950s. The dependence we are said to experience in response to the mysterium tremendum will not furnish us an answer to the vexing question of how to live in accordance with the external will; reverence will not tell us what to do for God. Piety may give us an impulse toward right action, a desire to do the best, but how do we determine what the best is? Nor is love sufficient — "And you shall love your neighbor" — but love alone will not tell us what to do for our neighbor when we love him; it is impossible to derive details of right conduct from love alone.

Religion, he writes, begins with embarrassment — but it doesn't stop there. Religion means challenge, not complacency. Challenge means overcoming "our adjustment to conventional notions, to mental clichés." Challenge means "maladjustment" as "a prerequisite for an authentic awareness of that which is."

To be maladjusted was also intellectual for my father: to think independently, critically, never to be satisfied with an *answer or an argument, but constantly to question and strive for something deeper. And of course, maladjustment was key to the prophetic life: refusing to accept inequality, the status quo, cruelties, and suffering.*

Philosophers of religion have a tendency to ignore religion and construct a philosophical edifice that they then dissect, searching for the pathology of unwarranted claims. Religious beliefs and practices are usually omitted from philosophical studies of religion, with the consequence that the historical and cultural context of those beliefs and practices are neglected. Some Jewish theologians, such as Hermann Cohen, search for a pure set of Jewish beliefs, purged of superstitions, mysticisms, apocalypticisms, and focused instead on "ethical monotheism." Scholars of Judaism are often reconcilers: Ephraim Urbach, in his study of rabbinic thought, wades through numerous conflicting rabbinic positions to define a unified conclusion that he then compares favorably with the teachings of classical Greek philosophy.

By contrast, Judaism for my father is a living religion, not a philosophical abstract. It is from his experience growing up surrounded, as he writes, by people of "religious nobility" that he extracted his insights into the varied dimensions of religiosity. Most striking, he never seeks to reconcile conflicting theological issues, but instead insists on holding them in tandem, as though the tension between them is precisely what generates their vitality. Halakha, Jewish law, is in tension with aggada, Jewish theology; only together does Judaism come to life — and only when the two are in proper balance: too much halakha leads to what he called "religious behaviorism," while neglect of halakha in favor of aggada robs Judaism of its architecture and leads to collapse.

Similarly, religion, he writes, begins with embarrassment — but doesn't stop there. Without challenge — the divine demand for our action — religion will have no significance. A religious person is never satisfied but is always striving: intellectually and spiritually, but also on behalf of other people, nature, and for the sake of God.

To be maladjusted was intellectual for my father: to think independently, critically, never to be satisfied with an answer or an argument, but constantly question and strive for something deeper. He never fully "fit in" to the contexts in which he lived and taught, but was always more or less maladjusted, questioning the intellectual and political consensus. And of course, maladjustment was key to the prophetic life: refusing to accept inequality, the status quo, cruelties, and suffering.

What is tragic in my life I have only the power to conceal. What is romantic I could not suppress but only distort. I was often lyric in spite of my fears. My real ambition was to sing thoughts with precision, to remain tender in the midst of inward panic. My ultimate goal was to bid us all to hear that God lives, loves, and hears in spite of his utter hiddenness.   — *Unpublished manuscript*

TO RECOVER THE QUESTIONS

It is customary to blame secular science and antireligious philosophy for the eclipse of religion in modern society. It would be more honest to blame religion for its own defeats. Religion declined not because it was refuted, but because it became irrelevant, dull, oppressive, insipid. When faith is completely replaced by creed, worship by discipline, love by habit; when the crisis of today is ignored because of the splendor of the past; when faith becomes an heirloom rather than a living fountain; when religion speaks only in the name of authority rather than with the voice of compassion — its message becomes meaningless.

Religion is an answer to man's ultimate questions. The moment we become oblivious to ultimate questions, religion becomes irrelevant, and its crisis sets in. The primary task of philosophy of religion is to rediscover the questions to which religion is an answer. The inquiry must proceed both by delving into the consciousness of man as well as by delving into the teachings and attitudes of the religious tradition.

There are dead thoughts and there are living thoughts. A dead thought has been compared to a stone which one may plant in the soil. Nothing will come out. A living thought is like a seed. In the process of thinking, an answer without a question is devoid of life.

It may enter the mind; it will not penetrate the soul. It may become a part of one's knowledge; it will not come forth as a creative force....

In our quest for forgotten questions, the method and spirit of philosophical inquiry are of greater importance than theology, which is essentially descriptive, normative, and historical. Philosophy may be defined as the art of asking the right questions. One of the marks of philosophical thinking is that, in contrast to poetry, for example, it is not a self-sufficing pouring forth of insight but rather the explicit statement of a problem and the attempt to offer an answer to a problem. Theology starts with dogmas; philosophy begins with problems. Philosophy sees the problem first; theology has the answer in advance. We must not, however, disregard another important difference. Not only are the problems of philosophy not identical with the problems of religion; their status is not the same. Philosophy is, in a sense, a kind of thinking that has a beginning but no end. In it, the awareness of the problem outlives all solutions. Its answers are questions in disguise; every new answer giving rise to new questions. In religion, on the other hand, the mystery of the answer hovers over all questions. Philosophy deals with problems as universal issues; to religion the universal issues are personal problems. Philosophy, then, stresses the primacy of the problem, religion stresses the primacy of the person.

The fundamentalists claim that all ultimate questions have been answered; the logical positivists maintain that all ultimate questions are meaningless. Those of us who share neither the conceit of the former nor the unconcern of the latter, and reject both specious answers and false evasions, know that an ulti-mate issue is at stake in our existence, the relevance of which surpasses all final formulations. It is this embarrassment that is the starting point for our thinking. — *GSM*, 3–4

ROOSTER

A person wakes up one day and maintains that he is a rooster. We do not know what he means and assign him to an insane asylum. But when a person wakes up one day and maintains that he is a human being, we also do not know what he means.

Assuming that the earth were endowed with psychic power, it would raise the questions: Who is he — the strange intruder who clips my wings, who trims my gardens? He who cannot live without me and is not quite a part of me?

There are many facets and facts of my being of which I am aware and which remain peripheral and irrelevant to the under-standing of my existence. What upsets me most is: What is the meaning of my being? — *WIM*, 51–52

WONDER

As civilization advances, the sense of wonder declines. Such decline is an alarming symptom of our state of mind. Mankind will not perish for want of information, but only for want of appreciation. The beginning of our happiness lies in the under-standing that life without wonder is not worth living. What we lack is not a will to believe but a will to wonder.

Awareness of the divine begins with wonder. It is the result of what man does with his higher incomprehension. The greatest hindrance to such awareness is our adjustment to conventional notions, to mental clichés. Wonder or radical amazement, the state of maladjustment to words and notions, is therefore a prerequisite for an authentic awareness of that which is.

Radical amazement has a wider scope than any other act of man. While any act of perception or cognition has as its object a selected segment of reality, radical amazement refers to all of reality; not only to what we see, but also to the very act of seeing as well as to our own selves, to the selves that see and are amazed at their ability to see.

The grandeur or mystery of being is not a particular puzzle to the mind, as, for example, the cause of volcanic eruptions. We do not have to go to the end of reasoning to encounter it. Grandeur or mystery is something with which we are confronted everywhere and at all times. Even the very act of thinking baffles our thinking, just as every intelligible fact is, by virtue of its being a fact, drunk with baffling aloofness. Does not mystery reign within reasoning, within perception, within explanation? Where is the self-understanding that could unfurl the marvel of our own thinking, that could explain the grace of our emptying the concrete with charms of abstraction? What formula could explain and solve the enigma of the very fact of thinking? Ours is neither thing nor thought but only the subtle magic blending the two.

What fills us with radical amazement is not the relations in which everything is embedded but the fact that even the minimum of perception is a maximum of enigma. The most incomprehensible fact is the fact that we comprehend at all.

The way to faith leads through acts of wonder and radical amazement. The words addressed to Job apply to every man:

Hearken unto this, O Job,
Stand still and consider the wondrous works of the Lord.
Do you know how God lays His command upon them,
And causes the lightning of His cloud to shine?
Do you know the balancings of the clouds,
The wondrous works of Him who is perfect in knowledge,

You whose garments are hot when the earth is still because
    of the south wind?
Can you, like Him, spread out the skies,
Hard as a molten mirror?
Teach us what we shall say to Him;
We cannot draw up our case because of darkness.
Shall it be told Him that I would speak?
Did a man ever wish that he would be swallowed up?
And now men cannot look on the light
When it is bright in the skies
When the wind has passed and cleared them.
Out of the north comes golden splendor;
God is clothed with terrible majesty. (Job 37:14–22)

— *GSM*, 46–47

NATURE

According to the Bible, the "inner" life of nature is closed to man. The Bible does not claim that things speak to man; it only claims that things speak to God. Inanimate objects are dead in relation to man; they are alive in relation to God. They sing to God. The mountains melt like wax, the waters tremble at the presence of the Lord (Psalm 77:17; 97:5). "Tremble, O earth, at the presence of the Lord, at the presence of the God of Jacob" (Psalm 114:7).

Whose ear has heard the trees sing to God? Has our reason ever thought of calling upon the sun to praise the Lord? And yet, what the ear fails to perceive, what reason fails to conceive, the Bible makes clear to our souls. It is a higher truth, to be grasped by the spirit.

Modern man dwells upon the order and power of nature; the prophets dwell upon the grandeur and creation of nature. The former directs his attention to the manageable and intelligible aspect of the universe; the latter to the mystery and marvel.

What the prophets sense in nature is not a direct reflection of God but an allusion to Him. Nature is not a part of God but rather a fulfillment of His will.

Lift up your eyes on high and see who created these. There is a higher form of seeing. We must learn how to lift up our eyes on high in order to see that the world is more a question than an answer. The world's beauty and power are as naught compared to Him. The grandeur of nature is only the beginning. *Beyond the grandeur is God.*   — GSM, 97

EMBARRASSMENT

Let not the wise man glory in his wisdom, let not the mighty man glory in his might; but let him who glories glory in this: that he has a *sense of ultimate embarrassment.* How embarrassing for man to be the greatest miracle on earth and not to understand it! How embarrassing for man to live in the shadow of greatness and to ignore it, to be a contemporary of God and not to sense it. Religion depends upon what man does with his ultimate embarrassment. It is the awareness that the world is too great for him, the awareness of the grandeur and mystery of being, the awareness of being present at the unfolding of an inconceivable eternal saga.

Embarrassment is the awareness of an incongruity of character and challenge, of perceptivity and reality, of knowledge and understanding, of mystery and comprehension. Experiencing the evanescence of time, one realizes the absurdity of man's sense of sovereignty. In the face of the immense misery of the human species, one realizes the insufficiency of all human effort to relieve it. In the face of one's inner anguish, one realizes the fallacy of absolute expediency.

Embarrassment is a response to the discovery that in living we either replenish or frustrate a wondrous expectation. It involves an awareness of the grandeur of existence that may be wasted, of a waiting ignored, of unique moments missed. It is a protection against the outburst of the inner evils, against arro-gance, *hybris*, self-deification. The end of embarrassment would be the end of humanity.

There is hardly a person who does not submit his soul to the beauty parlor, who does not employ the make-up of vanity in order to belie his embarrassment. It is only before God that we all stand naked.

Great is the challenge we face at every moment, sublime the occasion, every occasion. Here we are, contemporaries of God, some of His power at our disposal.

The honest man is humbled by the awareness that his highest qualities are but semiprecious; all ground for firmness is mud. Except for his will to cling to life, what is his abiding concern?

Embarrassment not only precedes religious commitment; it is the touchstone of religious existence. How embarrassing for man to have been created in the likeness of God and to be unable to recognize him! In the words of Job:

> Lo, He passes by me and I see Him not;
> He moves on, but I do not perceive Him.
> (Job 9:11)

The sense of embarrassment may be contrasted with the self-assurance of a nonreligious type: "I do not need a God to tell me how to live. I am a good person without going to the syn-agogue or church." A religious man could never say: "I am a good person." Far from being satisfied with his conduct, he prays three times daily: "Forgive us, our Father, for we have sinned."

I am afraid of people who are never embarrassed at their own pettiness, prejudices, envy, and conceit, never embarrassed at the profanation of life. A world full of grandeur has been converted into a carnival. There are slums, disease, and star-vation all over the world, and we are building more luxurious hotels in Las Vegas. Social dynamics is no substitute for moral responsibility.

I shudder at the thought of a society ruled by people who are absolutely certain of their wisdom, by people to whom everything in the world is crystal-clear, whose minds know no mystery, no uncertainty.

What the world needs is a sense of embarrassment. Modern man has the power and the wealth to overcome poverty and disease, but he has no wisdom to overcome suspicion. We are guilty of misunderstanding the meaning of existence; we are guilty of distorting our goals and misrepresenting our souls. We are better than our assertions, more intricate, more profound than our theories maintain. Our thinking is behind the times.

What is the truth of being human? The lack of pretension, the acknowledgment of opaqueness, shortsightedness, inadequacy. But truth also demands rising, striving, for the goal is both within and beyond us. The truth of being human is gratitude; its secret is appreciation.   — *WIM*, 112–14

THE THREE DIMENSIONS

The concern for others is not an extension in breadth but an ascension, a rise. Man reaches a new vertical dimension, the dimension of the holy, when he grows beyond his self-interests, when that which is of interest to others becomes vital to him, and it is only in this dimension, in the understanding of its perennial validity, that the concern for other human beings and the devotion to ideals may reach the degree of self-denial. Distant ends, religious, moral, and artistic interests, may become as relevant to man as his concern for food. The self, the fellow-man and the dimension of the holy are the *three* dimensions of a mature human concern.   —*MNA*, 139

THE MEANING OF AWE

Awe is a way of being in rapport with the mystery of all reality. The awe that we sense or ought to sense when standing in the presence of a human being is a moment of intuition for the likeness of God which is concealed in his essence. Not only man; even inanimate things stand in a relation to the Creator. The secret of every being is the divine care and concern that are invested in it. Something is at stake in every event.

Awe is an intuition for the creaturely dignity of all things and their preciousness to God; a realization that things not only are what they are but also stand, however remotely, for something absolute. Awe is a sense for the transcendence, for the reference everywhere to Him who is beyond all things. It is an insight better conveyed in attitudes than in words. The more eager we are to express it, the less remains of it.

The meaning of awe is to realize that life takes place under wide horizons, horizons that range beyond the span of an individual life or even the life of a nation, a generation, or an era. Awe enables us to perceive in the world intimations of the divine, to sense in small things the beginning of infinite significance, to sense the ultimate in the common and the simple; to feel in the rush of the passing the stillness of the eternal.

In analyzing or evaluating an object, we think and judge from a particular point of view. The psychologist, economist, and chemist pay attention to different aspects of the same object. Such is the limitation of the mind that it can never see three sides of a building at the same time. The danger begins when, completely caught in one perspective, we attempt to consider a part as the whole. In the twilight of such perspectivism, even the sight of the part is distorted. What we cannot comprehend by analysis, we become aware of in awe. When we "stand still and consider," we face and witness what is immune to analysis.

Knowledge is fostered by curiosity; wisdom is fostered by awe. True wisdom is participation in the wisdom of God. Some people may regard as wisdom "an uncommon degree of common sense." To us, wisdom is the ability to look at all things from the point of view of God, sympathy with the divine pathos, the identification of the will with the will of God.

"Thus says the Lord: Let not the wise man glory in his wisdom, let not the mighty man glory in his might, let not the rich man glory in his riches; but let him who glories glory in this, that he understands and knows Me, that I am the Lord who practices kindness, justice, and righteousness on the earth; for in these things I delight, says the Lord" (Jeremiah 9:33–23).

—*MNA*, 139

Awe precedes faith; it is *at the root of faith.* We must grow in awe in order to reach faith. We must be guided by awe to be worthy of faith. Awe rather than faith is the cardinal attitude of the religious Jew. It is "the beginning and gateway of faith, the first precept of all, and upon it the whole world is established." In Judaism, *yirat hashem,* the awe of God, or *yirat shamayim,* the "awe of heaven," is almost equivalent to the word "religion." In Biblical language the religious man is not called "believer," as he is for example in Islam (*mu'min*), but *yirei hashem.*   —*GSM*, 75

RADICAL AMAZEMENT

The greatest hindrance to knowledge is our adjustment to conventional notions, to mental clichés. Wonder or radical amazement, the state of maladjustment to words and notions, is, therefore, a prerequisite for an authentic awareness of that which is.

Standing eye to eye with being as being, we realize that we are able to look at the world with two faculties — with reason and with wonder. Through the first we try to explain or to adapt the world to our concepts, through the second we seek to adapt our minds to the world.

Wonder rather than doubt is the root of knowledge. Doubt comes in the wake of knowledge as a state of vacillation between two contrary or contradictory views, as a state in which a belief we had embraced begins to totter. It challenges the mind's accounts about reality and calls for an examination and verification of that which is deposited in the mind. In other words, the business of doubt is one of auditing the mind's accounts about reality rather than a concern with reality itself; it deals with the content of perception rather than with perception itself.

Doubt is not applied to that which we have an immediate awareness of. We do not doubt that we exist or that we see; we merely question whether we know what we see or whether that which we see is a true reflection of what exists in reality. Thus, it is after perception has been crystallized in a conception that doubt springs up.

Doubt, then, is an interdepartmental activity of the mind. First we see; next we judge and form an opinion and thereafter we doubt. In other words, to doubt is to question that which we have accepted as possibly true a moment ago. Doubt is an act of appeal, a proceeding by which a logical judgment is brought from the memory to the critical faculty of the mind for re-examination. Accordingly, we must first judge and cling to a belief in our judgment before we are able to doubt. But if we must know in order to question, if we must entertain a belief in order to cast doubt upon it, then doubt cannot be the beginning of knowledge.

Wonder goes beyond knowledge. We do not doubt that we doubt, but we are amazed at our ability to doubt, amazed at our ability to wonder. He who is sluggish will berate doubt; he who is blind will berate wonder. Doubt may come to an end; wonder lasts forever. Wonder is a state of mind in which we do not look at reality through the latticework of our memorized knowledge, in which nothing is taken for granted. Spiritually we cannot live by merely reiterating borrowed or inherited knowledge. Inquire of your soul what does it know, what does it take for granted. It will tell you only no-thing is taken for granted; each thing is a surprise; *being is unbelievable.* We are amazed at seeing anything at all, amazed not only at particular values and things but *at the unexpectedness of being as such,* at the fact that there is being at all.　　　　　　　　　　　　　　　—*MNA*, 11–12

2

Prophecy Is the Voice That God
Has Lent to the Silent Agony

My father's doctoral dissertation, written at the University of
Berlin, was a study of prophetic consciousness. He reviewed the
biblical scholarship of the era, written mostly by German Protestants, and found that the approach failed to understand the
subjective experience of the prophets. He set out not to write
a history of the prophets, but to develop a phenomenological
method for understanding the nature of the prophetic experience. What was it to experience being a prophet? How did
the prophets experience God's call and message? What is the
purpose of prophecy?

While the era of classical prophecy had ended, the teachings
of the prophets and the nature of prophetic experience of the
divine continued, with important lessons for the present day. It
was in the spirit of the prophets that my father became involved
in the civil rights movement. His telegram to President Kennedy,
responding to an invitation to join religious leaders for a meeting at the White House, makes clear that concrete action was
essential, inspired by "moral grandeur and spiritual audacity."
When my father was invited to a conference in Chicago in
1963, organized by the National Conference of Christians and
Jews, on the topic "Religion and Race," he insisted that they
were two words that should never be uttered together: they

were diametrically opposed. Religion joins together, race tears asunder.

Those were years of tremendous challenge. My father was one of the first to speak out on behalf of Soviet Jews, who were not permitted to practice Judaism, and he became involved in negotiations with Vatican representatives during the Second Vatican Council, which was preparing a statement on the church's relations with the Jewish people. The escalating war in Vietnam horrified him, and he founded an organization, Clergy and Laymen Concerned about Vietnam, to mobilize a religious movement to stop the war.

Throughout, one can hear echoes of the Holocaust and the lessons he drew from it. The silence of German clergy during the Third Reich, the mass, mindless enthusiasm for Hitler, the vicious anti-Semitism, all shaped my father's response to the horrors of the postwar era. While the Holocaust is a silent presence in much of my father's writings, he spoke explicitly on occasion, and it was linked to his passionate efforts to liberate Jews from the Soviet Union. As his brief prayer indicates, he enjoined American Jews not to forget nor to be indifferent to the plight of the Russian Jews. On one occasion, when my father spoke together with Martin Luther King Jr. to a convention of synagogue leaders about Soviet Jewry, my father ended with a brief and very moving speech about the Holocaust that he delivered in Yiddish.

His friendship with Martin Luther King Jr. remained strong and vibrant. One of the great questions of the mid-1960s was whether Dr. King should speak out against the war in Vietnam. When he did, on April 4, 1967, at Riverside Church in New York, my father introduced him. A year later, Dr. King spoke to a convention of Conservative rabbis, gathered at the Concord Hotel, in honor of my father, and again my father introduced him.

War is not only a political issue, but a moral issue. Opposition to the war in Vietnam was rooted in my father's understanding of the Bible, especially the prophets, and their central teaching for him was compassion. The indifference of so many Americans to the slaughter and destruction of that war horrified him; Vietnam, he wrote, "is a personal problem. To speak about God and remain silent on Vietnam is blasphemous." Ultimately, he wrote in some unpublished notes that conclude this chapter, sin is "abuse of freedom." God is filled with compassion, concern, and pathos, whereas the tragedy of human beings is their indifference and impartiality; the root of sin is callousness.

WHAT MANNER OF MAN IS THE PROPHET?

The prophet is a man who feels fiercely. God has thrust a burden on his soul, and he is bowed and stunned at man's fierce greed. Frightful is the agony of man; no human voice can convey its full terror. Prophecy is the voice that God has lent to the silent agony, a voice to the plundered poor, to the profaned riches of the world. It is a form of living, a crossing point of God and man. God is raging in the prophet's words....

Above all, the prophets remind us of the moral state of a people: Few are guilty, but all are responsible. If we admit that the individual is in some measure conditioned or affected by the spirit of society, an individual's crime discloses society's corruption. In a community not indifferent to suffering, uncompromisingly impatient with cruelty and falsehood, continually concerned for God and every man, crime would be infrequent rather than common.

To a person endowed with prophetic sight, everyone else appears blind; to a person whose ear perceives God's voice, everyone else appears deaf. No one is just; no knowing is strong enough, no trust complete enough. The prophet hates the approximate; he shuns the middle of the road. Man must live on the summit to avoid the abyss. There is nothing to hold to except God. Carried away by the challenge, the demand to straighten out man's ways, the prophet is strange, one-sided, an unbearable extremist.

Others may suffer from the terror of cosmic aloneness; the prophet is overwhelmed by the grandeur of divine presence. He is incapable of isolating the world. There is an interaction between man and God which to disregard is an act of insolence. Isolation is a fairy tale.

Where an idea is the father of faith, faith must conform to the ideas of the given system. In the Bible the realness of God came first, and the task was how to live in a way compatible with His presence. Man's coexistence with God determines the course of history.

The prophet disdains those for whom God's presence is comfort and security; to him it is a challenge, an incessant demand. God is compassion, not compromise; justice, though not inclemency. The prophet's predictions can always be proved wrong by a change in man's conduct, but never the certainty that God is full of compassion.

The prophet's word is a scream in the night. While the world is at ease and asleep, the prophet feels the blast from heaven.

The prophet faces a coalition of callousness and established authority and undertakes to stop a mighty stream with mere words. Had the purpose been to express great ideas, prophecy would have had to be acclaimed as a triumph. Yet the purpose of prophecy is to conquer callousness, to change the inner man as well as to revolutionize history.

It is embarrassing to be a prophet. There are so many pretenders, predicting peace and prosperity, offering cheerful words, adding strength to self-reliance, while the prophet predicts disaster, pestilence, agony, and destruction. People need exhortations to courage, endurance, confidence, fighting spirit, but Jeremiah proclaims: You are about to die if you do not have a change of heart and cease being callous to the word of God. He sends shudders over the whole city, at a time when the will to fight is most important.

By the standards of ancient religions, the great prophets were rather unimpressive. The paraphernalia of nimbus and evidence, such as miracles, were not at their disposal....

The words the prophet utters are not offered as souvenirs. His speech to the people is not a reminiscence, a report, hearsay. The prophet not only conveys; he reveals. He almost does unto others what God does unto him. In speaking, the prophet reveals God. This is the marvel of a prophet's work: in his words, *the invisible God becomes audible.* He does not prove or argue. The thought he has to convey is more than language can contain. Divine power bursts in his words. The authority of the prophet is in the Presence his words reveal.

There are no proofs for the existence of the God of Abraham. There are only witnesses. The greatness of the prophet lies not only in the ideas he expressed, but also in the moments he experienced. The prophet is a witness, and his words a testimony — to *His* power and judgment, to *His* justice and mercy.

—*Prophets*, 5–6, 19–20, 27

TELEGRAM TO PRESIDENT JOHN F. KENNEDY

WHITE HOUSE
I LOOK FORWARD TO PRIVILEGE OF BEING PRESENT AT MEET-ING TOMORROW FOUR PM. LIKELIHOOD EXISTS THAT NEGRO PROBLEM WILL BE LIKE WEATHER. EVERYBODY TALKS ABOUT IT BUT NOBODY DOES ANYTHING ABOUT IT. PLEASE DEMAND OF RELIGIOUS LEADERS PERSONAL INVOLVEMENT NOT JUST SOLEMN DECLARATION. WE FORFEIT RIGHT TO WORSHIP GOD AS LONG AS WE CONTINUE TO HUMILIATE NEGROES. CHURCH SYNAGOGUE HAVE FAILED, THEY MUST REPENT. ASK OF RELIGIOUS LEADERS TO CALL FOR NATIONAL REPENTANCE AND PERSONAL SACRI-FICE. LET RELIGIOUS LEADERS DONATE ONE MONTH'S SALARY TOWARD FUND FOR NEGRO HOUSING AND EDUCATION. I PRO-POSE THAT YOU MR. PRESIDENT DECLARE STATE OF MORAL

EMERGENCY. A MARSHALL PLAN FOR AID TO NEGROES IS BECOM-
ING A NECESSITY. THE HOUR CALLS FOR MORAL GRANDEUR AND
FOR SPIRITUAL AUDACITY.

ABRAHAM JOSHUA HESCHEL

RELIGION AND RACE

At the first conference on religion and race, the main participants were Pharaoh and Moses. Moses' words were: "Thus says
the Lord, the God of Israel, let My people go that they may
celebrate a feast to Me." While Pharaoh retorted: "Who is the
Lord, that I should heed this voice and let Israel go? I do not
know the Lord, and moreover I will not let Israel go."

The outcome of that summit meeting has not come to an end.
Pharaoh is not ready to capitulate. The exodus began but is far
from having been completed. In fact, it was easier for the children of Israel to cross the Red Sea than for a Negro to cross
certain university campuses.

Let us dodge no issues. Let us yield no inch to bigotry, let us
make no compromise with callousness.

In the words of William Lloyd Garrison, "I will be as harsh
as truth and as uncompromising as justice. On this subject
[slavery] I do not wish to think, to speak, or to write with mod-
eration. I am in earnest — I will not equivocate — I will not
excuse — I will not retreat a single inch — and I will be heard."

Religion and race. How can the two be uttered together? To
act in the spirit of religion is to unite what lies apart, to remember that humanity as a whole is God's beloved child. To act in
the spirit of race is to sunder, to slash, to dismember the flesh
of living humanity. Is this the way to honor a father: to torture his child? How can we hear the word "race" and feel no
self-reproach?

Race as a *normative* legal or political concept is capable
of expanding to formidable dimensions. A mere thought, it
extends to become a way of thinking, a highway of insolence, as

well as a standard of values, overriding truth, justice, beauty. As a standard of values and behavior, race operates as a comprehensive doctrine, as racism. And racism is worse than idolatry. *Racism is satanism,* unmitigated evil.

Few of us seem to realize how insidious, how radical, how universal and evil racism is. Few of us realize that racism is man's gravest threat to man, the maximum of hatred for a minimum of reason, the maximum of cruelty for a minimum of thinking.

Perhaps this conference should have been called "Religion *or* Race." You cannot worship God and at the same time look at man as if he were a horse.

Shortly before he died, Moses spoke to his people, "I call heaven and earth to witness against you this day: I have put before you life and death, blessing and curse. *Choose life"* (Deuteronomy 30:19). The aim of this conference is first of all to state clearly the stark alternative. I call heaven and earth to witness against you this day: I have set before you religion and race, life and death, blessing and curse. Choose life.

"Race prejudice, a universal human ailment, is the most recalcitrant aspect of the evil in man" (Reinhold Niebuhr), a treacherous denial of the existence of God.

What is an idol? *Any god who is mine but not yours,* any god concerned with me but not with you, *is an idol.*

Faith in God is not simply an *afterlife-insurance policy. Racial or religious bigotry* must be recognized for what it is: *satanism, blasphemy.*

In several ways man is set apart from all beings created in six days. The Bible does not say, God created the plant or the animal; it says, God created *different* kinds of plants, *different kinds* of animals (Genesis 1:11–12, 21–25). In striking contrast, it does not say, God created different kinds of man, men of different colors and races, it proclaims, God created one single man. From one single man all men are descended.

To think of a man in terms of white, black, or yellow is more than an error. It *is an eye disease, a cancer of the soul.*

The redeeming quality of man lies in his ability to sense his kinship with all men. Yet there is a deadly poison that inflames the eye, making us see the generality of race but not the uniqueness of the human face. Pigmentation is what counts. The Negro is a stranger to many souls. There are people in our country whose moral sensitivity suffers a blackout when confronted with the black man's predicament.

How many disasters do we have to go through in order to realize that all of humanity has a stake in the liberty of one person; whenever one person is offended, we are all hurt. What begins as inequality of some inevitably ends as inequality of all.

In referring to the Negro in this paper we must, of course, always keep equally in mind the plight of all individuals belonging to a racial, religious, ethnic, or cultural minority.

This conference should dedicate itself not only to the problem of the Negro but also to the problem of the white man, not only to the plight of the colored but also to the situation of the white people, to the cure of a disease affecting the spiritual substance and condition of every one of us. What we need is an NAAAP, a National Association for the Advancement of All People. Prayer and prejudice cannot dwell in the same heart. Worship without compassion is worse than self-deception; it is an abomination.

Thus the problem is not only how to do justice to the colored people; it is also how to stop the profanation of God's name by dishonoring the Negro's name.

One hundred years ago the emancipation was proclaimed. It is time for the white man to strive for *self-emancipation,* to set himself free of bigotry, to stop being a slave to wholesale contempt, a passive recipient of slander.

"Again I saw all the oppressions that are practiced under the sun. And behold, the tears of the oppressed, and they had no one to comfort them!" (Ecclesiastes 4:1)....

My heart is sick when I think of the anguish and the sighs, of the quiet tears shed in the nights in the overcrowded dwellings in the slums of our great cities, of the pangs of despair, of the cup of humiliation that is running over....

Let us cease to be apologetic, cautious, timid. Racial tension and strife is both sin and punishment. *The Negro's plight,* the blighted areas in the large cities, are they not the fruit of our sins?

By negligence and silence we have all become accessory before the God of mercy to the injustice committed against the Negroes by men of our nation. Our derelictions are many. We have failed to demand, to insist, to challenge, to chastise.

In the words of Thomas Jefferson, "I tremble for my country when I reflect that God is just...."

Who shall plead for the helpless? Who shall prevent the epidemic of injustice that no court of justice is capable of stopping?

In a sense, the calling of the prophet may be described as that of an advocate or champion, speaking for those who are too weak to plead their own cause. Indeed, the major activity of the prophets was *interference,* remonstrating about wrongs inflicted on other people, meddling in affairs which were seemingly neither their concern nor their responsibility. A prudent man is he who minds his own business, staying away from questions which do not involve his own interests, particularly when not authorized to step in — and prophets were given no mandate by the widows and orphans to plead their cause. The prophet is a person who is not tolerant of wrongs done to others, who resents other people's injuries. He even calls upon others to be champions of the poor. It is to every member of the community, not alone to the judges, that Isaiah directs his plea:

> Seek justice, relieve the oppressed,
> Judge the fatherless, plead for the widow.
> (Isaiah 1:17)

The prophets' great contribution to humanity was the discovery of *the evil of indifference.* One may be decent and sinister, pious and sinful.

In condemning the clergymen who joined Dr. Martin Luther King Jr. in protesting against local statutes and practices which denied constitutional liberties to groups of citizens on account of race, a white preacher declared: "The job of the minister is to lead the souls of men to God, not to bring about confusion by getting tangled up in transitory social problems."

In contrast to this definition, the prophets passionately proclaim that God himself is concerned with "the transitory social problems," with the blights of society, with the affairs of the market place.

What is the essence of being a prophet? *A prophet is a person who holds God and men in one thought at one time, at all times.* Our tragedy begins with *the segregation of God*, with the bifurcation of the secular and sacred. We worry more about the purity of dogma than about the *integrity of love. We think of God in the past tense* and refuse to realize that *God is always present* and *never, never past*; that God may be more intimately *present in slums than in mansions; with those who are smarting under the abuse of the callous.*

There are, of course, many among us whose record in dealing with the Negros and other minority groups is unspotted. However, an honest estimation of the moral state of our society will disclose: *some are guilty, but all are responsible.* If we admit that the individual is in some measure conditioned or affected by the public climate of opinion, an individual's crime discloses society's corruption. In a community not indifferent to suffering, uncompromisingly impatient with cruelty and falsehood, racial discrimination would be infrequent rather than common.

That equality is a good thing, a fine goal, may be generally accepted. What is lacking is a sense of the *monstrosity of inequality.* Seen from the perspective of prophetic faith, the predicament of justice is the predicament of God.

Of course, more and more people are becoming aware of the Negro problem, but they fail to grasp its being a personal problem. People are increasingly fearful of social tension and disturbance. However, so long as our society is more concerned to prevent racial strife than to prevent humiliation, the cause of strife, its moral status will be depressing, indeed.

The history of interracial relations is a nightmare. Equality of all men, a platitude to some minds, remains a scandal to many hearts. Inequality is the ideal setting for the abuse of power, a perfect justification for man's cruelty to man. Equality is an obstacle to callousness, setting a limit to power. Indeed, the history of mankind may be described as the history of the tension between power and equality.

Equality is an interpersonal relationship, involving both a claim and a recognition. My claim to equality has its logical basis in the recognition of my fellow men's identical claim. Do I not forfeit my own rights by denying to my fellow men the rights I claim for myself?

It is not humanity that endows the sky with inalienable stars. It is not society that bestows upon every man his inalienable rights. Equality of all men is not due to man's innocence or virtue. Equality of man is due to *God's love and commitment to all men.*

The ultimate worth of man is due neither to his virtue nor to his faith. *It is due to God's virtue, to God's faith. Wherever you see a trace of man, there is the presence of God.* From the perspective of eternity our recognition of equality of all men seems as generous an act as the acknowledgment that stars and planets have a right to be.

How can I withhold from others what does not belong to me?

Equality as a religious commandment goes beyond the principle of equality before the law. Equality as a religious commandment means *personal involvement,* fellowship, mutual reverence and concern. It means my being hurt when a Negro is offended. It means that I am bereaved whenever a Negro is *disenfranchised....*

There is no insight more disclosing: *God is One, and humanity is one.* There is no possibility more frightening: God's name may be desecrated.

God is every man's pedigree. He is either the Father of all men or of no man. The image of God is either in every man or in no man....

You shall not make yourself a graven image or any likeness of God. The making and worshiping of images in considered an abomination, vehemently condemned in the Bible. The world and God are not of the same essence. There can be no man-made symbols of God.

And yet there is something in the world that the Bible does regard as a symbol of God. It is not a temple or a tree; it is not a statue or a star. *The symbol of God is man,* every man. How significant is the fact that the term *tselem,* which is frequently used in a damnatory sense for a man-made image of God, as well as the term *demuth,* likeness — of which Isaiah claims (40:18) no *demuth* can be applied to God — are employed in denoting man as a image and likeness of God. Man, every man, must be treated with the honor due to a likeness representing the King of Kings.

There are many motivations by which prejudice is nourished, many reasons for despising the poor, for keeping the underprivileged in his place. However, the Bible insists that the interests of the poor have precedence over the interests of the rich. The prophets have a bias in favor of the poor....

The way we act, the way we fail to act is a disgrace, which must not go on forever. This is not a white man's world. This is not a colored man's world. It is God's world. No man has a place in this world who tries to keep another man in his place. It is time for the white man to repent. We have failed to use the avenues open to us to educate the hearts and minds of men, to identify ourselves with those who are underprivileged. But repentance is more than contrition and remorse for sins, for harms done. Repentance means a new insight, a new spirit. It also means a course of action.

Racism is an evil of tremendous power, but God's will transcends all powers. Surrender to despair is surrender to evil. It is important to feel anxiety; it is sinful to wallow in despair.

What we need is a total mobilization of heart, intelligence, and wealth for the purpose of love and justice. God is in search of man, waiting, hoping for man to do His will.

The most practical thing is not to weep but to act and to have faith in God's assistance and grace in our trying to do His will.

This world, this society can be redeemed. God has a stake in our moral predicament. I cannot believe that God will be defeated.

What we face is a human emergency. It will require much devotion, wisdom, and divine grace to eliminate that massive sense of inferiority, the creeping bitterness. It will require a high quality of imaginative sympathy, sustained cooperation both in thought and in action, by individuals as well as by institutions, to weed out memories of frustration, roots of resentment.

We must act even when inclination and vested interests would militate against equality. Human self-interest is often our Nemesis! It is the audacity of faith that redeems us. To have faith is to be ahead of one's normal thoughts, to transcend confused motivations, to lift oneself by one's bootstraps. Mere knowledge or belief is too feeble to be a cure of man's hostility to man, of man's tendency to fratricide. The only remedy is *personal sacrifice*: to abandon, to reject what seems dear and even plausible for the sake of the greater truth; to do more than one is ready to understand for the sake of God. Required is a breakthrough, a *leap of action*. It is the deed that will purify the heart. It is the deed that will sanctify the mind. The deed is the test, the trial and the risk.

The plight of the Negro must become our most important concern. Seen in the light of our religious tradition, *the Negro problem is God's gift to America,* the test of our integrity, a magnificent spiritual opportunity.

Humanity can thrive only when challenged, when called upon to answer new demands, to reach out for new heights. Imagine how smug, complacent, vapid, and foolish we would be if we had to subsist on prosperity along. It is for us to understand that religion is not sentimentality, that God is not a patron. Religion is a demand; God is a challenge, speaking to us in the language of human situations. His voice is in the dimension of history.

The universe is done. The greater masterpiece still undone, still in the process of being created, is history. For accomplishing His grand design, God needs the help of man. Man is and has the instrument of God, which he may or may not use in consonance with the grand design. Life is clay, and righteousness the mold in which God wants history to be shaped. But human beings, instead of fashioning the clay, deform the shape. God needs mercy, righteousness; His needs cannot be satisfied in space, by sitting in pews, by visiting temples, but in history, in time. It is within the realm of history that man is charged with God's mission.

There are those who maintain that the situation is too grave for us to do much about it, that whatever we might do would be "too little too late," that the most practical thing we can do is "to weep" and to despair. If such a message is true, then God has spoken in vain.

Such a message is four thousand years too late. It is good Babylonian theology. In the meantime, certain things have happened: Abraham, Moses, the Prophets, the Christian Gospel.

History is not all darkness. It was good that Moses did not study theology under the teachers of that message; otherwise, I would still be in Egypt building pyramids. Abraham was all alone in a world of paganism; the difficulties he faced were hardly less grave than ours.

The greatest heresy is despair, despair of men's power for goodness, men's power for love.

It is not enough for us to exhort the Government. What we must do is to set an example, not merely to acknowledge the Negro but to welcome him, not grudgingly but joyously, to take delight in enabling him to enjoy what is due to him. We are all *Pharaohs* or *slaves of Pharaohs*. It is sad to be a slave of Pharaoh. *It is horrible to be a Pharaoh.*

Daily we should take account and ask: What have I done today *to alleviate the anguish, to mitigate the evil, to prevent humiliation?*

Let there be a grain of prophet in every man!

Our concern must be expressed not symbolically, but literally; not only publicly, but also *privately;* not only occasionally, but regularly.

What we need is the involvement of every one of us as individuals. What we need is restlessness, a constant awareness of the monstrosity of injustice.

The concern for the dignity of the Negro must be an explicit tenet of our creeds. He who offends a Negro, whether as a landowner or employer, whether as waiter or salesgirl, is guilty of offending the majesty of God. No minister or layman has a right to question the principle that reverence for God is shown in reverence for man, that the fear we must feel lest we hurt or humiliate a human being must be as unconditional as fear of God. An act of violence is an act of desecration. To be arrogant toward man is to be blasphemous toward God.

In the words of Pope John XXIII, when opening the Twenty-first Ecumenical Council, "Divine Providence is leading us to a new order of human relations." History has made us all neighbors. The age of moral mediocrity and complacency has run out. This is a time for radical commitment, for radical action.

Let us not forget the story of the sons of Jacob. Joseph, the dreamer of dreams, was sold into slavery by his own brothers. But at the end it was Joseph who rose to be the savior of those who had sold him into captivity.

Mankind lies groaning, afflicted by fear, frustration, and despair. Perhaps it is the will of God that among the Josephs of the future there will be many who have once been slaves and whose skin is dark. The great spiritual resources of the Negroes, their capacity for joy, their quiet nobility, their attachment to the Bible, their power of worship and enthusiasm, may prove a blessing to all mankind.

In the words of the prophet Amos (5:24):

> Let justice roll down like waters,
> and righteousness like a mighty stream.

A mighty stream, expressive of the vehemence of a never-ending, surging, fighting movement — as if obstacles had to be washed away for justice to be done. No rock is so hard that water cannot pierce it. "But the mountain falls and crumbles away, and the rock is removed from its place; the waters wear away the stones" (Job 14:18f.). Justice is not a mere norm, but a fighting challenge, a restless drive.

Righteousness as a mere tributary, feeding the immense stream of human interests, is easily exhausted and more easily abused. But righteousness is not a trickle; it is God's power in the world, a torrent, an impetuous drive, full of grandeur and majesty. The surge is choked, the sweep is blocked. Yet the mighty stream will break all dikes.

Justice, people seem to agree, is a principle, a norm, an ideal of the highest importance. We all insist that it ought to be — but it may not be. In the eyes of the prophets, justice is more than an idea or a norm: justice is charged with the omnipotence of God. What ought to be, shall be! — *IF,* 85–100

TO DESPAIR IS TO BETRAY

To us of this generation who have walked through the ruins of aborted dreams and desecrated ideals and have arrived at the gate of the seventies of the twentieth century, the supreme question is: How does the road sign read: Abandon all hope, ye who enter here. Or: To despair is to betray; at the end His mercy will prevail.

The one road sign may be almost everywhere, the other road sign is revealed in the lives of those who would rather suffer than bear falsehood, who would rather be exposed to torture and living in jail than to remain silent in the face of lies, blasphemy, and injustice. — *Unpublished manuscript*

AFTER MAJDANEK

We still feel the blow to our head. It feels like the heavens above us have fallen in chunks. We have not yet grasped the disaster that has befallen us. We are still before the funeral — still prepared to sit *shiva* confounded, confused, and petrified.

How do we endure this? How do we bear the pain? Are we idiots? Are we base? When I think of my people, burned and cremated in Poland, a shudder courses through my veins. I feel the nails of insanity.

I choke on pain and drive away from myself the picture, the sound, the woe. No, one cannot drive away an ocean; one can bury oneself in a hole, a pit of forgetfulness.

How worthless is such a life in hiding. The sound of the ocean roars in the distance, there is nowhere to run away. Our misfortune is large as God. We mask the sound of the shudder with cheap noisemakers. Talk is a waste of time; we won't experience any good fortune (and even saying these words is foolish). We have Tisha B'Av all year and yet — we put on Purim plays.

When every happiness is a bitter mockery for us. Whom are we fooling?

Eloquence is not possible, no exaggerations in our outcry, in our mourning and tears. Who can describe "how a nation was burned"?

When we were blinded by the light of European civilization, we could not appreciate the value of the small fire of our eternal light. In the spiritual confusion of the last hundred years, many of us overlooked the incomparable beauty of our old, poor home. We compared our fathers and grandfathers, our teachers and rabbis, with Russian or German intellectuals. We preached in the name of the twentieth century, compared Berdichev to Paris, Ger with Heidelberg. Dazzled by big city street lamps, we lost our inner vision. The luminous visions that for so many generations shone in the little candles were extinguished for many of us.

Now, trampled and bloodied in the light of the blinding lamps of civilization and evil, we sense the importance of our small candles which our mothers so piously blessed.

— "After Majdanek: On Aaron Aaron Zeitlin's New Poems," originally published in *Yidisher Kemfer* 29, no. 771 (October 1, 1948), trans. Morris M. Faierstein

OUR AFTERLIFE

What should have been our answer to Auschwitz? Should this people, called to be a witness to the God of mercy and compassion, persist in its witness and cling to Job's words: "Even if He slay me yet will I trust in Him" (Job 13:15), or should this people follow the advice of Job's wife, "Curse God and die!" (Job 2:9), immerse itself into the anonymity of a hundred nations all over the world, and disappear once and for all?

Our people's faith in God at this moment in history did not falter. At this moment in history Isaac was indeed sacrificed, his blood shed. We all died in Auschwitz, yet our faith survived. We knew that to repudiate God would be to continue the Holocaust. We have once lived in a civilized world, rich in trust and expectation. Then we all died, were condemned to dwell in hell. Now we are living in hell. Our present life is our afterlife....

We did not blaspheme, we built. Our people did not sally forth in flight from God. On the contrary, at that moment in history we saw the beginning of a new awakening, the emergence of a new concern for a Living God theology. Escape from Judaism giving place increasingly to a new attachment, to a rediscovery of our legacy....

For these many ages, in many lands, whether in Spain or in India, in Egypt or in Poland, no day, no evening passes without praying for Zion and Jerusalem. We pray for her recovery, we pray for her redemption, for her prosperity, and for her peace. ...We have never abandoned the land, and it is as if the land has never abandoned the Jewish people....

As a hope, as a dream, as an article of faith, it lived in the hearts of the Jews of all ages.

Auschwitz is in our veins. It abides in the throbbing of our hearts. It burns in our imagination, it trembles in our conscience....

What would be the face of Western history today if the end of twentieth-century Jewish life would have been Bergen-Belsen, Dachau, Auschwitz? The State of Israel is not an atonement. It would be blasphemy to regard it as a compensation. However, the existence of Israel reborn makes life less unendurable. It is a slight hinderer of hindrances to believing in God.... And yet, there is no answer to Auschwitz.... To try to answer is to commit a supreme blasphemy. Israel enables us to bear the agony of Auschwitz without radical despair, to sense a ray of God's radiance in the jungles of history.

How do you live in the city of God?

The heart of the relationship between God and human beings is reciprocity, interdependence. The task is to humanize the sacred and to sanctify the secular.   — *Israel, passim*

KADDISH FOR OUR SOULS

The excerpt below is one of the rare moments when my father spoke directly about the Shoah. The occasion was a lecture he delivered in 1963 at a gathering of Conservative synagogue leaders at the Concord Hotel in the Catskills. Martin Luther King Jr. also delivered an address that evening, and both of them spoke about the effort to free Soviet Jews. My father had only recently met Dr. King, at a conference in Chicago, and his speech at the Concord reiterated many of the same themes he addressed there: that religion is incompatible with radical prejudice; that religion is the opposite of indifference. At the very end of his speech, my father switched to Yiddish, explaining, "East European Jewry has vanished. Let us not repeat the sin we have committed and let us not let the rest vanish. I would like to spend the next three minutes by saying just a few words to you in Yiddish in honor of the Russian Jews, most of whom still speak Yiddish. I'd like to say something about our inner situation in relation to what happened in our times, in the early 1940s."

We still feel the blow to our head. Huge chunks are falling from the heavens, but we have yet to grasp the rupture and the misfortune that have befallen us. We are still waiting for the funeral, not yet ready to sit *shiva*. Distraught, broken, confused, and petrified, we are living in a state of chaos. We celebrate our joyous occasions, but it's akin to holding a wedding ceremony at a cemetery.

Our enjoyments are awkward and even grotesque, mere this-worldly pleasures. Our people was consumed by fire. And the world is unchanged. The ash of human skeletons emits no odor. The atmosphere of the world is not contaminated. Our bread is fresh; our sugar is sweet. The screams of millions of victims of the crematoria were never transmitted over the radio waves. Hush, quiet; nothing ever happened. If we still had a heart, then it has turned to stone. I often sit and wonder: perhaps our souls went up in flames along with their bodies in Majdanek and Auschwitz.

Ours is Godless world. We Jews dance around the Golden Calf. We have forgotten that we live in a world that is *treyf* (impure). The times are dark, yet we do not even light the Sabbath candles. Six million Jews went up in smoke. Blood will remain silent. But our conscience is mute as a wall. We are inebriated and distracted by the follies of this world. The martyrs do not need our recitations of *kaddish* — but we need someone to recite *kaddish* over us, for us, because we have lost our souls.

I do not seek merely to unburden my heart. We will not fulfill our obligation by reciting lamentations. Our task is not to bang our heads against the wall. Our task is to find an answer to a crucial question: What is our generation's obligation? What is the task? Not to forget, never to be indifferent to other people's suffering.   — *Unpublished manuscript*, translated from the Yiddish by Sylvia Fuks Fried

PRAYER FOR SOVIET JEWS

Although Stalin's death in 1953 had eased some of the overt persecutions of Jews in the Soviet Union, Jews still could not practice their religion or study Hebrew freely, and they were afraid to gather at synagogues to pray.

My father's call to rescue the Jews of Soviet Russia began early and was passionate — and not always well received in the early years by Jewish leaders who felt that quiet diplomacy was the best political route with the Soviet Union. In September 1963, my father delivered a strong speech to a gathering of rabbis at the Jewish Theological Seminary, a speech my mother urged him to tone down, knowing he would be criticized sharply for it. "What is called for is not a silent sigh but a voice of moral compassion and indignation, the sublime and inspired screaming of a prophet uttered by a whole community," he stated. Deeply aware of the silence of many American Jews during the Holocaust just twenty years earlier, my father warned, "We have been guilty more than once of failure to be concerned, of a failure to cry out, and failure may have become our habit."

The Free Soviet Jewry movement quickly became a force to reckon with in the United States, both for American Jews and within the American political landscape.

I found this prayer on behalf of Jews in the Soviet Union among my father's files, written in his hand on a scrap of paper. There is no date and no indication of where he offered the prayer.

This morning we prayed for Soviet Jews.
Now let us pray for the Jews of America, for ourselves.
Prayer has meaning: the beginning of commitment, the
    starting point of personal involvement.
May our concern of this moment not be ephemeral.

Save us from indifference, from moral lethargy.

Let us help one another to retain an awareness of the
    nightmare, the Jewish situation in Soviet Russia,
Lest we forget,
Lest we forget.
Lest we betray our sacred commitment.

Foster a sense of indebtedness.
Let us turn the sense of fear into a sense of embarrassment.
Let us turn the fellowship of fear into a fellowship of
    embarrassment.
What have we done with our power!

— Unpublished manuscript

INTRODUCTION TO MARTIN LUTHER KING AT RIVERSIDE (1967)

On April 4, 1967, one year to the day before he was assassinated, Martin Luther King spoke out forcefully against the war in Vietnam in a speech entitled, "To Redeem the Soul of America," delivered at Riverside Church in New York City.

Sponsoring the event was an organization called Clergy and Laymen Concerned about Vietnam (CALCAV), which my father played a major role in establishing. In 1965, he and a few other clergy leaders held a press conference to protest the war in Vietnam: John Bennett, president of Union Theological Seminary, Father Daniel Berrigan, Rev. William Sloane Coffin, chaplain of Yale University, Lutheran Pastor Richard John Neuhaus, and

Reform Rabbi Balfour Brickner. At the end of the press confer-
ence, one of the reporters asked, "But what are you going to do
with your protests?"

My father replied, "We are forming an organization of clergy
and laymen concerned about Vietnam." The others were sur-
prised, not having discussed this, but CALCAV went on to
become a major force in the antiwar movement, largely thanks
to its brilliant executive director, Richard Fernandez. Its motto
was, "A Time to Break the Silence."

The question of whether Dr. King should speak out against
the war in Vietnam was vigorously discussed at the time, and I
remember the sense of moral urgency. If Dr. King were to speak
out, how would it affect the civil rights movement, particularly
support from Congress and the president? After much reflection
and discussion, Dr. King came to the decision that he should
speak out against the war, for which he came under widespread
attack. Introducing Dr. King at Riverside Church that evening
in 1967, my father made this statement:

The state requires that the citizen risk his life for it; the acceptance
of sacrifice is one of our essential duties, but it is also the duty of
the citizen, who, after careful study, becomes convinced that a
war his country is involved in is both morally wrong and politi-
cally absurd, to do his utmost to stop it. Except anguish and love
of America we have no other feelings. Our thoughts on Vietnam
are sores, destroying our trust, ruining our most cherished commitments with burdens of shame. We are pierced to the core with
pain, and it is our duty as citizens to say no to the subversiveness
of our government, which is ruining the values we cherish. The
American promise [means] to say no to a policy which moves
from folly to madness. The blood we shed in Vietnam makes
a mockery of all our proclamations, dedications, celebrations.
Has our conscience become a fossil, is all mercy gone? If mercy,
the mother of humility, is still alive as a demand, how can we
say yes to our bringing agony to that tormented country? We
are here because our own integrity as human beings is decaying

in the agony and merciless killing done in our name. In a free society, some are guilty and all are responsible. We are here to call upon the governments of the United States as well as North Vietnam to stand still and to consider that no victory is worth the price of terror, which all parties commit in Vietnam, north and south. Remember that blood of the innocent cries forever. Should that blood stop to cry, humanity would cease to be.

INTRODUCTION TO MARTIN LUTHER KING AT CONCORD (1968)

The editor of Conservative Judaism *introduced this transcription with the following headnote: "On the evening of March 25, 1968, ten days before he was killed, Dr. Martin Luther King appeared at the sixty-eighth annual convention of the Rabbinical Assembly. He responded to questions which had been submitted in advance to Rabbi Everett Gendler, who chaired the meeting.*

"Here is a transcript of what was said that evening, beginning with the words of Professor Abraham Joshua Heschel, who presented Dr. King to the assembled rabbis."

The poignant "conversation" took place in the afterglow of Rabbi Abraham Joshua Heschel's introduction of Dr. King before his fellow rabbis and foreshadowed the broken civil rights alliance between many Jewish and African American leaders.

Where does moral religious leadership in America come from today? The politicians are astute, the establishment is proud, and the market place is busy. Placid, happy, merry, the people pursue their work, enjoy their leisure, and life is fair. People buy, sell, celebrate, and rejoice. The fail to realize that in the midst of our affluent cities there are districts of despair, areas of distress.

Where does God dwell in America today? Is He at home with those who are complacent, indifferent to other people's agony, devoid of mercy? Is He not rather with the poor and the contrite in the slums?

Dark is the world for me, for all its cities and stars. If not for the few signs of God's radiance, who could stand such agony, such darkness?

Where in America today do we hear a voice like the voice of the prophets of Israel? Martin Luther King is a sign that God has not forsaken the United States of America. God has sent him to us. His presence is the hope of America. His mission is sacred, his leadership of supreme importance to every one of us.

The situation of the poor in America is our plight, our sickness. To be deaf to their cry is to condemn ourselves.

Martin Luther King is a voice, a vision, and a way. I call upon every Jew to harken to his voice, to share his vision, to follow in his way. The whole future of America will depend upon the impact and influence of Dr. King.

May everyone present give of his strength to this great spiritual leader, Martin Luther King.

TOWARD A JUST SOCIETY: PRAYER

Vietnam is a personal problem. To speak about God and remain silent on Vietnam is blasphemous.

> *When you spread forth your hands*
> *I will hide my eyes from you;*
> *Yea, when you make many prayers,*
> *I will not hear —*
> *Your hands are not clean.*

In the sight of so many thousands of civilians and soldiers slain, injured, crippled, of bodies emaciated, of forests destroyed by fire, God confronts us with this question: Where are you? Is there no compassion in the world? No sense of discernment to realize that this is a war that refutes any conceivable justification of war? The sword is the pride of man; arsenals, military bases, nuclear weapons lend supremacy to nations. War is the climax of ingenuity, the object of supreme dedication. Men slaughtering each other, cities battered into ruins: such insanity has plunged many nations into an abyss of disgrace.

Will America, the promise of peace to the world, fail to uphold its magnificent destiny?

The most basic way in which all men may be divided is between those who believe that war is unnecessary and those who believe that war is inevitable; between those to whom the sword is the symbol of honor and those to whom seeking to convert swords into plowshares is the only way to keep our civilization from disaster.

Most of us prefer to disregard the dreadful deeds we do over there. The atrocities committed in our name are too horrible to be credible. It is beyond our power to react vividly to the ongoing nightmare, day after day, night after night. So we bear graciously other people's suffering.

O Lord, we confess our sins, we are ashamed of the inadequacy of our anguish, of how faint and slight is our mercy. We are a generation that has lost the capacity for outrage. We must continue to remind ourselves that in a free society all are involved in what some are doing. *Some are guilty; all are responsible.*

Prayer is our greatest privilege. To pray is to stake our very existence, our right to live, on the truth and on the supreme importance of that which we pray for. Prayer, then, is radical commitment, a dangerous involvement in the life of God. In such awareness we pray....   —*MGSA*, 231

WHAT IS SIN?

What is a sin? The abuse of freedom. A failure in depth, failure to respond to God's challenge.

The root of sin is callousness, hardness of heart, lack of understanding what is at stake in being alive.

Not ultimate, irreducible condition, but disturbance in relationship between God and man.

There is an evil which most of us condone and are even guilty of: indifference to evil. We remain neutral, impartial, and not easily moved by the wrongs done unto other people.

Indifference to evil is more insidious than evil itself; it is more universal, more contagious, more dangerous.

A silent justification, it makes possible an evil erupting as an exception becoming the rule and being in turn accepted.

The knowledge of evil is something which the first man acquired; it was not something that the prophets had to discover. Their great contribution to humanity was the discovery of the evil of indifference. One may be decent and sinister, pious and sinful. I am my brother's keeper.

The prophet is a person who suffers the harm done to others.

Wherever a crime is committed, it is as if the prophet were the victim and the prey. The prophet's angry words cry. The wrath of God is a lamentation.

All prophecy is one great exclamation: God is not indifferent to evil!

God is always concerned. He is personally affected by what man does to man. He is a God of pathos. This is one of the meanings of the anger of God: the end of indifference! The message of wrath is frightful, indeed. But for those who have been driven to the brink of despair by the sight of what malice and ruthlessness can do, comfort will be found in the thought that evil is not the end, that evil is never the climax of history. This is the most vexing question in a world where the righteous suffer and the wicked prosper: Does God condone? Does God care for right and wrong? If the agony of man were a form of serenity, a mild assertion — a work of divine commiseration, a word of reprobation — would have been adequate. To a generation afflicted by the fury of cruel men, by the outrage of abandoning God, no condemnation is too harrowing.

Man's sense of injustice is a poor analogy to God's sense of injustice. The exploitation of the poor is to us a misdemeanor;

to God, it is a disaster. Our reaction is disapproval, God's reaction is something no language can convey.

Man is what he thinks. Man dwells where his mind dwells. What is intellectually irrelevant is imprisoned in Temples and has no access to our minds.

We repeat clichés; we remember platitudes.

God is presented to us as a comfort, not a challenge, a rumor, as if it is nice to have Him around. But God means defiance, rejection, as well as affirmation.

We have relinquished our role as educators. We surrender, we abandon, we desert, and we forget.

— Unpublished manuscript

3

God Is Not Silent.
He Has Been Silenced

A Hasidic rebbe once asked, rhetorically, "Where is God?" And he answered, "Wherever we let Him in."

The old Jewish doctrine of God hiding from us, and hence allowing evil to flourish, has at times been invoked as a response to the Holocaust and the question of theodicy: How can we justify a good God in the face of so much evil? By contrast, my father sees the central question as anthropodicy: How could human beings commit mass murder? How can God continue to have faith in our humanity, given the wickedness we commit?

God is always present, he believed, but we human beings fail to allow Him to enter. "God did not depart of His own volition; He was expelled" (MNA, 153). We have placed God in exile and as a result, "the mark of Cain on the face of man has come to overshadow the likeness of God." Unlike Søren Kierkegaard, my father did not view faith as a "teleological suspension of the ethical." Rather, "faith is an event," a challenge, because faith has consequences, and what is important is not simply having an awareness of God's presence, but what we do with that awareness.

God may be hiding, concealed by human beings, but is actually "waiting to be disclosed, to be admitted into our lives." In such moments, heaven and earth kiss each other.

Elsewhere, though, my father writes of God's constant presence: "God follows me everywhere," he declares in a poem; "We do not think Him, we are stirred by Him," he writes in God in Search of Man *(160). There may be a wall, an abyss, a labyrinth, but those are human creations that can be overcome. God is listening, but we are enclosed in "shells of ambition, of vanity, of infatuation with success." It is in moments of anguish, brokenheartedness, when we abandon self-reflection and think of God, making God immanent and present, that we realize God's subjectivity and begin to pray.*

This section begins with excerpts from my father's two major books, Man Is Not Alone *and* God in Search of Man, *and includes an English translation of a Yiddish poem he wrote at the age of twenty, while living in Vilnius. The section also includes excerpts from two lectures he delivered on prayer, one at the Protestant Union Theological Seminary, in 1958, the other to Conservative rabbis a few years later. Each of them carries a message that can easily be understood by both Christians and Jews.*

THE HIDING GOD

For us, contemporaries and survivors of history's most terrible horrors, it is impossible to meditate about the compassion of God without asking: Where is God?

Emblazoned over the gates of the world in which we live is the escutcheon of the demons: the mark of Cain on the face of man has come to overshadow the likeness of God. There has never been so much distress, agony, and terror. It is often sinful for the sun to shine. At no time has the earth been so soaked with blood. Fellowmen have turned out to be evil spirits, monstrous and weird. Does not history look like a stage for the dance of might and evil — with man's wits too feeble to separate the two and God either directing the play or indifferent to it?

The major folly of this view seems to lie in its shifting the responsibility for man's plight from man to God, in accusing the Invisible though iniquity is ours. Rather than admit our own guilt, we seek, like Adam, to shift the blame upon someone else. For generations we have been investing life with ugliness and now we wonder why we do not succeed. God was thought of as a watchman hired to prevent us from using our loaded guns. Having failed us in this, He is now thought of as the ultimate Scapegoat.

We live in an age when most of us have ceased to be shocked by the increasing breakdown in moral inhibitions. The decay of conscience fills the air with a pungent smell. Good and evil, which were once as distinguishable as day and night, have become a blurred mist. But that mist is man-made. God is not silent. He has been silenced.

Instead of being taught to answer the direct commands of God with a conscience open to His will, men are fed on the sweetness of mythology, on promises of salvation and immortality as a dessert to the pleasant repast on earth. The faith believers cherish is second hand: it is a faith in the miracles of the past, an attachment to symbols and ceremonies. God is known from hearsay, a rumor fostered by dogmas, and even nondogmatic thinkers offer hackneyed, solemn concepts without daring to cry out the startling vision of the sublime on the margin of which indecisions, doubts, are almost vile.

We have trifled with the name of God. We have taken ideals in vain, preached and eluded Him, praised and defied Him. Now we reap the fruits of failure. Through centuries His voice cried in the wilderness. How skillfully it was trapped and imprisoned in the temples! How thoroughly distorted! Now we behold how it gradually withdraws, abandoning one people after another, departing from their souls, despising their wisdom. The taste for goodness has all but gone from the earth.

We have witnessed in history how often a man, a group, or a nation, lost from the sight of God, acts and succeeds, strives and achieves, but is given up by Him. They may stride from one victory to another and yet they are done with and abandoned, renounced and cast aside. They may possess all glory and might, but their life will be dismal. God has withdrawn from their life, even while they are heaping wickedness upon cruelty and malice upon evil. The dismissal of man, the abrogation of Providence, inaugurates eventual calamity.

They are left alone, neither molested by punishment nor assured by indication of help. The divine does not interfere with their actions nor intervene in their conscience. Having all in abundance save His blessing, they find their wealth a shell in which there is curse without mercy.

Man was the first to hide himself from God (Genesis 3:8), after having eaten of the forbidden fruit, and is still hiding (Job 13:20–24). The will of God is to be here, manifest and near; but when the doors of this world are slammed on Him, His truth betrayed, His will defied, He withdraws, leaving man to himself. God did not depart of His own volition; He was expelled. *God is in exile.*

More grave than Adam's eating the forbidden fruit was his hiding from God after he had eaten it. "Where art thou?" Where is man? is the first question that occurs in the Bible. It is man's alibi that is our problem. It is man who hides, who flees, who has an alibi. God is less rare than we think; when we long for Him, His distance crumbles away.

The prophets do not speak of the *hidden* God but of *hiding* God. His hiding is a function not His essence, an act, not a permanent state. It is when the people forsake Him, breaking the Covenant which He has made with them, that He forsakes them and hides His face from them (Deuteronomy 31:16–17). It is not God who is obscure. It is man who conceals Him. His hiding from us is not in His essence: "Verily Thou art a God that hidest Thyself, O God of Israel, the Saviour!" (Isaiah 45:15). A hiding God, not a hidden God. He is waiting to be disclosed, to be admitted into our lives.

The direct effect of His hiding is the hardening of the conscience: man hears but does not understand, sees but does not perceive — his heart fat, his ears heavy (Isaiah 6).

Our task is to open our souls to Him, to let Him again enter our deeds. We have been taught the grammar of contact with God; we have been taught by the Baal Shem that His remoteness is an illusion capable of being dispelled by our faith. There are many doors through which we have to pass in order to enter the palace, and none of them is locked.

As the hiding of man is known to God and seen through, so is God's hiding seen through. In sensing the fact of His hiding we have disclosed Him. Life is a hiding place for God. We are never asunder from Him who is in need of us. Nations roam and rave — but all this is only ruffling the deep, unnoticed, and uncherished stillness.

The grandchild of Rabbi Baruch was playing hide-and-seek with another boy. He hid himself and stayed in his hiding place for a long time, assuming that his friend would look for him. Finally, he went out and saw that his friend was gone, apparently not having looked for him at all, and that his own hiding had been in vain. He ran into the study of his grandfather, crying and complaining about his friend. Upon hearing the story, Rabbi Baruch broke into tears and said: "God, too, says: 'I hide, but there is no one to look for me.'"

There are times when defeat is all we face, when horror is all that faith must bear. And yet, in spite of anguish, in spite of terror we are never overcome with ultimate dismay. "Even that it would please God to destroy me; that He would let loose His hand and cut me off, then should I yet have comfort, yea, I would exult even in my pain; let Him not spare me, for I have not denied the words of the holy One" (Job 6:9–10). Wells gush forth in the deserts of despair. This is the guidance of faith: "Lie in the dust and gorge on faith."   —*MNA*, 151–55

GOD FOLLOWS ME EVERYWHERE

God follows me everywhere,
Weaves a net of glances around me,
Dazzles my blind back like a sun.

God follows me everywhere like a forest.
My lips are constantly astonished, heartfelt-mute,
Like a child stumbling upon an ancient shrine.

God follows me everywhere like a shudder.
I yearn for rest, but within me sounds the call: "Come!
See how visions linger in the streets."

I stroll about my thoughts like a mystery,
Down a long corridor through the world,
And sometimes high above I see the faceless face of God.

•

God follows me in trams, in cafés —
Oh, only with the backs of my pupils can I see
How mysteries arise, how visions transpire!

> — *The Ineffable Name of God: Man,* 23,
> dedicated to my teacher Dovid Koigen,
> translation © Jeffrey Shandler.

GOD IS THE SUBJECT

The sense for the realness of God will not be found in insipid concepts; in opinions that are astute, arid, timid; in love that is scant, erratic. Sensitivity to God is given to a broken heart, to a mind that rises above its own wisdom. It is a sensitivity that bursts all abstractions. It is not a mere playing with a notion. There is no conviction without contrition; no affirmation without self-engagement. Consciousness of God is a response, and God is a challenge rather than a notion. We do not think Him;

we are stirred by Him. We can never describe Him; we can only
return to Him. We may address ourselves to Him; we cannot
comprehend Him. We can sense His presence; we cannot grasp
His essence.

His is the call, ours the paraphrase; His is the creation, ours
a reflection. He is not an object to be comprehended, a thesis to
be endorsed; neither the sum of all that is (facts) nor a digest of
all that ought to be (ideals). He is the ultimate subject.

The trembling sense for the hereness of God is the assumption of our being accountable to Him. God-awareness is not an
act of God being known to man; it is the awareness of man's
being known by God. In thinking about Him we are thought
by him.   — GSM, 159–60

FAITH IS AN EVENT

Men have often tried to give itemized accounts of why they
must believe that God exists. Such accounts are like ripe fruit
we gather from the trees. Yet it is beyond all reasons, beneath
the ground, where a seed starts to become a tree, that the act of
faith takes place.

The soul rarely knows how to raise its deeper secrets to dis-
cursive levels of the mind. We must not, therefore, equate the
act of faith with its expression. The expression of faith is an
affirmation of truth, a definite judgment, a conviction, while
faith itself is *an event,* something that happens rather than
something that is stored away; it is *a moment* in which the soul
of man communes with the glory of God.

Man's walled mind has no access to a ladder upon which he
can, on his own strength, rise to knowledge of God. Yet his soul
is endowed with translucent windows that open to the beyond.
And if he rises to reach out to Him, it is a reflection of the
divine light in him that gives him the power for such yearning.
We are at times ablaze against and beyond our own power, and

unless man's soul is dismissed as an insane asylum, the spectrum analysis of that ray is evidence for the truth of his insight.

For God is not always silent, and man is not always blind. His glory fills the world; His spirit hovers above the waters. There are moments in which, to use a Talmudic phrase, heaven and earth kiss each other, in which there is a lifting of the veil at the horizon of the known, opening a vision of what is eternal in time. Some of us have at least once experienced the momentous realness of God. Some of us have at least caught a glimpse of the beauty, peace, and power that flow through the souls of those who are devoted to Him. There may come a moment like thunder in the soul, when man is not only aided, not only guided by God's mysterious hand, but also taught how to aid, how to guide other beings. The voice of Sinai goes on forever: "These words the Lord spoke unto all your assembly in the mount out of the midst of the fire, of the cloud, and of the thick darkness, with *a great voice that goes on for ever.*"   —*GSM*, 138

PRAYER AS DISCIPLINE

The universe would be an inferno without a God who cares. There is no echo within the world for the agony and cry of humanity. There is only God who hears.

Consider the disproportion of misery and compassion. The depth of anguish is an abyss, its intricacies are a veritable labyrinth, and our grasp of it may be compared to the grasp of a butterfly flying over the Grand Canyon. Callousness, the dreadful incompatibility of existence and response, is man's outstanding failure. For the sin we have sinned in not knowing how much we sin; we cry for forgiveness. Dark is the world for me for all its cities and stars. If not for the certainty that God listens to our cry, who could stand so much misery, so much callousness?

The mystery and the grandeur of the concern of the infinite God for the finite man is the basic insight of biblical tradition. This mystery is enhanced by the aspect of immediacy. God is *immediately* concerned. He is not concerned through intermediate agents. He is personally concerned.

Prayer is more than a cry for the mercy of God. It is more than a spiritual improvisation. Prayer is a condensation of the soul. It is the whole soul in one moment, the quintessence of all our acts, the climax of all our thoughts. For prayer to live in man, man has to live in prayer. In a sense, prayer is a part of a greater issue. It depends upon the total moral and spiritual situation of man, it depends upon a mind within which God is at home. Of course, there are lives which are at the bottom too barren to bring forth a thought in the presence of God. If all the thoughts and anxieties of such people do not contain enough spiritual substance to be distilled into prayer, an inner transformation is a matter of emergency.

The only way we can discuss prayer is on the basis of self-reflection, trying to describe what has happened to us in a rare and precious moment of prayer. The difficulty of self-reflection consists in the fact that what is given to us is only a recollection. You cannot, of course, analyze the act of prayer while praying. To worship God means to forget the self, an extremely difficult, though possible, act. What takes place in a moment of prayer may be described as a shift of the center of living — from self-consciousness to self-surrender. This implies, I believe, an important indication of the nature of man. Prayer begins as an "it-He" relationship. I am not ready to accept the ancient concept of prayer as a dialogue. Who are we to enter a dialogue with God? The better metaphor would be to describe prayer as an act of immersion, comparable to the ancient Hebrew custom of immersing oneself completely in the waters as a way of self-purification to be done over and over again. Immersion in the waters! One feels surrounded, touched by the waters, drowned in the waters of mercy. In prayer the "I" becomes an "it." This is the discovery: what is an "I" to me, first of all and essentially, and "it" to God. If it is God's mercy that lends eternity to a speck of being which is usually described as a self, then prayer begins as a moment of living as an "it" in the presence of God. The closer to the presence of Him, the more obvious becomes the absurdity of the "I." The "I" is dust and ashes. "I am dust and ashes," says Abraham; then he goes on in dialogue to argue with the Lord about saving the cities of Sodom and Gomorrah. How does Moses at the burning bush respond to the call to go to the people of Israel and to bring them the message of redemption? "Who am I that I should go to Pharaoh and bring the children out of Egypt?" Only God says "I." This is how the Ten Commandments begin: "I am the Lord."

Prayer is a moment when humility is a reality. Humility is not a virtue. Humility is truth. Everything else is illusion. In other words it is not as an "I" that we approach God, but rather through the realization that there is only one "I." Now it is our being precious to Him that sets us apart from being merely an accidental by-product of the cosmic process. This is why in Jewish liturgy primacy is given to prayer of praise. One must never begin with supplication. One begins with praise because praise is the prerequisite and essence of prayer. To praise means to make Him present, to make present not only His power and splendor but also His mercy. His mercy and His power are one.

How does man become a person, an "I"? By becoming a thought of God. Man lives on earth as a self but also as an object of divine concern. Such discovery is the reward of prayer. Such realization is the major motivation in piety. This is the goal of the pious man: to become worthy to be remembered by God.

Thus the purpose of prayer is to be brought to God's attention: to be listened to, to be understood by Him. In other words, the true task of man is not to know God but to be known to God. Here lies the meaning of living according to religious discipline: to make our existence worthy of being known to God. This may not be the essence of grace, but it is the gate to grace.

Are we worthy of entering into His mercy, of being a matter of concern to Him? The answer is given in prayer. Prayer is the affirmation of the preciousness of man. Prayer may not save us, but it makes us worthy of being saved.

There is no human misery more strongly felt than the state of being forsaken by God. Nothing is more dreadful than rejection by Him. Rejection, being forsaken, living a life deserted by God, is possible. But it is the fear of being forgotten that is a powerful spur to a person to enter prayer, to bring himself to the attention of God. In prayer we learn that it is better to be smitten by His punishment than to be left alone. Perhaps all prayer may be summarized in one utterance: "Do not forsake us, O Lord."

Prayer is not speculation. In speculation, God is an object; to the man who prays, God is the subject. When awakening to the presence of God, we do not strive to acquire objective knowledge but to deepen a mutual allegiance. What we long for in such moments is not to know Him but to be known to Him; not to form judgments about Him but to be judged by Him; not to make the world an object of our mind but to augment His, rather than our, knowledge. We endeavor to disclose ourselves to the Sustainer of all rather than to enclose the world in ourselves.

To disclose the self we must learn how to cast off the shells of ambition, of vanity, of infatuation with success. We are all very poor, very naked, and rather absurd in our misery and in our success. We are constantly dying alive. From the view of temporality we are all dead except for a moment. There is only one bridge over the abyss of despair: prayer.

The presence of God is the absence of despair. In the stillness of sensing His presence misery turns to joy, despair turns to prayer. I repeat, prayer is more than a cry out of anguish. It is rather a moment of sensing His mercy. Let me make clear what I mean. A moment of supplication is an expression of what we need at the moment. A person may go on pondering deeply in intense emotion about his needs, about the need of the moment. That is not yet prayer. Adding "in the name of God" to it will not make it prayer. It is the cry of anguish which becomes a realization of God's mercy that constitutes prayer. It is the moment of a person in anguish forgetting his anguish and thinking of God and His mercy. That is prayer. Not self-reflection, but the direction of the entire person upon God. It is a difficult but not impossible situation. It may last a moment but it is the essence of a lifetime.

The true motivation for prayer is not, as it has been said, the sense of being at home in the universe, but rather the sense of not being at home in the universe. Is there a sensitive heart that could stand indifferent and feel at home in the sight of so much evil and suffering, in the face of countless failures to live up to the will of God? On the contrary, the experience of not being at home in the world is a motivation for prayer. That experience gains intensity in the amazing awareness that God himself is not at home in the universe. He is not at home in a universe where His will is defied and where His kingship is denied. God is in exile; the world is corrupt. The universe is not at home. To pray means to bring God back into the world, to establish His kingship for a second at least. To pray means to expand His presence. In the most important moment of the Jewish liturgy, we cry out of the depth of our disconcerted souls a prayer for redemption. "Lord our God, put Thy awe upon all whom Thou hast made, Thy dread upon whom Thou hast created, so that all Thy works may revere Thee, and all that Thou hast created may prostrate themselves before Thee, and all form one union to do Thy will wholeheartedly." To worship, therefore, means to make God immanent, to make Him present. His being immanent in the world depends upon us. When we say "Blessed be He," we extend His glory, we bestow His spirit upon the world. In other words, what underlies all this is not a mystic experience of our being close to Him but the certainty of His being close to us and of the necessity of His becoming closer to us.

Let me warn against the equating of prayer with emotion. Emotion is an important component of prayer, but the primary presupposition is conviction. If such conviction is lacking, if the presence of God is a myth, then prayer to God is a delusion. If God is unable to listen to us, then we are insane in talking to Him. All this presupposes conviction. The source of prayer then is an insight rather than an emotion. It is the insight into the mystery of reality; it is, first of all, the sense of the ineffable that enables us to pray. As long as we refuse to take notice of what is beyond our sight, beyond our reason, as long as we are blind to the mystery of being, the way to prayer is closed to us. If the rising of the sun is but a daily routine of nature there is no reason for us to praise the Lord for the sun and for the life we live. The way to prayer leads to acts of wonder and radical amazement. The illusion of total intelligibility, the indifference to the mystery that is everywhere, the foolishness of ultimate self-reliance, are serious obstacles on the way. It is in the moment of our being faced with the mystery of living and dying, of knowing and not knowing, of loving and the inability to love that we pray, that we address ourselves to Him who is beyond the mystery.   —IF, 254–59

ON PRAYER

For centuries Jerusalem lay in ruins; of the ancient glory of King David and Solomon only a wall remained, a stone wall left standing after the Temple was destroyed by Romans. For centuries Jews would go on a pilgrimage to Jerusalem in order to pour out their hearts at the Wailing Wall.

A wall stands between man and God, and at the wall we must pray, searching for a cleft, for a crevice, through which our words can enter and reach God behind the wall. In prayer we must often knock our heads against the stone wall. But God's silence does not go on forever. While man is busy setting up screens, thickening the wall, prayer may also succeed in penetrating the wall.

The tragedy is that many of us do not even know how to find the way leading to the wall. We of this generation are afflicted with a severe case of dulling or loss of vision. Is it the result of our own intoxication, or is it the result of God's deliberate concealment of visible lights?

The spiritual memory of many people is empty, words are diluted, incentives are drained, inspiration is exhausted. Is God to be blamed for all this? Is it not man who has driven Him out of our hearts and minds? Has not our system of religious education been an abysmal failure?

This spiritual blackout is increasing daily. Opportunism prevails, callousness expands, the sense of the holy is melting away. We no longer know how to resist the vulgar, how to say no in the name of a higher yes. Our roots are in a state of decay.

This is an age of spiritual blackout, a blackout of God. We have entered not only the dark night of the soul, but also the dark night of society. We must seek out ways of preserving the strong and deep truth of a living God theology in the midst of the blackout.

For the darkness is neither final nor complete. Our power is first in waiting for the end of darkness, for the defeat of evil; and our power is also in coming upon single sparks and occasional rays, upon moments full of God's grace and radiance.

We are called to bring together the sparks to preserve single moments of radiance and keep them alive in our lives, to defy absurdity and despair, and to wait for God to say again: Let there be light.

And there will be light.   —*MGSA*, 267

4

In the Realm of Spirit
Only He Who Is a Pioneer
Is Able to Be an Heir

During the 1950s and 1960s, American Jews exerted a strong effort at assimilation, with many abandoning Sabbath observance and assuming that Judaism was archaic and would soon disappear. Successful writers on religion argued that religion is useful — unites the community, calms tensions — and such approaches were particularly powerful in the Cold War era. Joshua Loth Liebman produced the first best-seller by a rabbi, Peace of Mind, *in 1946; for the Christians, there was Norman Vincent Peale's* The Power of Positive Thinking, *published in 1952. Religion was reduced to a tool of psychology, and psychology became the interpreter of the soul. Judaism was held slightly above Christian theology, based on the argument that we have no theology, that we can abstract our rituals and discard our belief, using Jewish observance as a tool to maintain the family and create community without the pathetic embarrassments of God, faith, and piety. Demystifying religion was seen as a therapy or liberation: belief in God was viewed as an illness, religion as false consciousness, collective neurosis, alienation. Such approaches, Van Harvey notes in* Feuerbach and the Interpretation of Religion *(231), leave us wondering why*

religion persists and why religious people derive great meaning, depth of experience, and profound insight from something sick, false, and alienating.

Soon, however, came a shift: in the 1970s and 1980s, American Jews began recovering their Jewish identity, with renewed religious observance, revived interest in Jewish history and literature, reclamation of Hebrew and Yiddish. Orthodoxy began to grow, the Chabad Hasidic movement gained adherents, and a new Jewish fundamentalism began to emerge.

While my father always encouraged Jews to become more engaged in Jewish study, observance, and prayer, he also warned against attempting to imitate previous generations — that, he said, would be "spiritual plagiarism," a loss of integrity and a destruction of Judaism's authenticity.

Judaism, he writes, is "spiritual effrontery," a religion of dissent. That means dissent from blind adherence to a collective mentality, but it also means dissent within Judaism: "creative dissent is not simply repudiation"; it offers a vision. My father never aligned himself with any of the denominations within Judaism, and he never labeled himself a "Conservative" or "Orthodox" Jew. Neither "obsolete liberalism or narrow parochialism" was satisfactory.

If Judaism is to be authentic, Jews must renounce imitation — not only of our grandparents' Judaism, but also of ourselves. Lack of sincerity makes Judaism inauthentic, but how do we achieve sincerity, if not through profound and continuous self-examination? These are ideas my father explored in relation to the Kotzker rebbe, a Hasidic rebbe of the nineteenth century, in his final two books, Kotzk, *a two-volume study in Yiddish, and* A Passion for Truth, *both published in 1973.*

Such self-examination is central to the preparation for Yom Kippur. In a short essay, based on a talk my father gave to some rabbis preparing for the High Holy Days, he describes the extraordinary awe he experienced as a young man in Warsaw, preparing for Yom Kippur, a day of fasting and repentance, a day in which we leave our human nature and become like angels: "There was no fear of punishment, not even a fear of death, but the expectation of standing in the presence of God."

What he doesn't mention in the article, but remains vivid to me, is how our family spent the evening that followed the conclusion of Yom Kippur. What should one do at the conclusion of Yom Kippur? We had just spent twenty-five hours fasting, most of that time in the synagogue, praying the most extraordinary liturgy of the Jewish year, and then my father, my mother, and I came home to our quiet apartment, drank some tea and talked, then ate a bit and talked some more. It was a contemplative, peaceful time, a time for recovery from the day but also of clinging to the awe of that day.

Discussions of Yom Kippur, or of Jewish education, or of the obligations of rabbis are not parochial, but can easily be relevant to Christians or to Muslims. Indeed, my father writes, "no religion is an island," each is affected by others. Attacks on Judaism are assaults on Christianity, and vice versa: "Jews must realize that the spokesmen of the Enlightenment who attacked Christianity were no less negative in their attitude toward Judaism." Each religion is bound up with others: millenarian movements that swept through Christian society triggered millenarian hopes among Jews as well, and false messianic movements within Islam prompted corresponding false messianic movements within Judaism.

For my father, however, the issue was not only sociological or historical influences, but something deeper: religions are not only about theology, but about depth theology, that level of fear and trembling in which faith comes to life. My father did not consider it helpful to discuss with Christians those issues that divide us, such as Christology, but to focus instead on the dimension of faith: "sharing insights, confessing inadequacy."

Concluding his inaugural lecture as Henry Emerson Fosdick Visiting Professor at Union Theological Seminary, he spoke these deeply moving words: "What, then, is the purpose of interreligious cooperation? It is neither to flatter not to refute one another, but to help one another; to share insight and learning, to cooperate in academic ventures on the highest scholarly level and, what is even more important, to search in the wilderness for wellsprings of devotion, for treasures of stillness, for the power of love and care for man. What is urgently needed are ways of helping one another in the terrible predicament of here and now by the courage to believe that the word of the Lord endures forever as well as here and now; to cooperate in trying to bring about a resurrection of sensibility, a revival of conscience; to keep alive the divine sparks in our souls, to nurture openness to the spirit of the Psalms, reverence for the words of the prophets, and faithfulness to the Living God."

FAITH AS AN INDIVIDUAL MEMORY

To have faith does not mean, however, to dwell in the shadow of old ideas conceived by prophets and sages, to live off an inherited estate of doctrines and dogmas. In the realm of spirit only he who is a pioneer is able to be an heir.* The wages of spiritual plagiarism is the loss of integrity; self-aggrandizement is self-betrayal.

Authentic faith is more than an echo of a tradition. It is a creative situation, an event. For God is not always silent, and man is not always blind. In every man's life there are moments when there is a lifting of the veil at the horizon of the known, opening a sight of the eternal. Each of us has at least once in his life experienced the momentous reality of God. Each of us has once caught a glimpse of the beauty, peace, and power that flow through the souls of those who are devoted to Him.

---

*The eighteen benedictions begin with the words: "Blessed by Thou O Lord, our God and the God of our fathers, the God of Abraham, the God of Issac, the God of Jacob." The question has been asked: Why is it necessary to specify the three names after having said "our fathers"? That repetition, the answer goes, serves to indicate that neither Issac nor Jacob relied entirely upon their fathers, but sought to find God themselves. This is why we speak of the God of Abraham, of Isaac, or Jacob. Rabbi Meir Eisenstadt, Panim Me'iroth, no. 39 (Amsterdam, 1715).

But such experiences or inspiration are rare events. To some
people they are like shooting stars, passing and unremembered.
In others they kindle a light that is never quenched. The remembrance of that experience and the loyalty to the response of that
moment are the forces that sustain our faith. In this sense, faith
is faithfulness, loyalty to an event, loyalty to our response.

— *MNA,* 164–65

DISSENT

Inherent to all traditional religion is the peril of stagnation.
What becomes settled and established may easily turn foul.
Insight is replaced by clichés, elasticity by obstinacy, spontaneity
by habit. Acts of dissent prove to be acts of renewal.

It is therefore of vital importance for religious people to voice
and to appreciate dissent. And dissent implies self-examination,
critique, discontent.

Dissent is indigenous to Judaism. The prophets of ancient
Israel who rebelled against a religion that would merely serve
the self-interest or survival of the people continue to stand out
as inspiration and example of dissent to this very day.

An outstanding feature dominating all Jewish books com-
posed during the first five hundred years of our era is the
fact that together with the normative view a dissenting view
is nearly always offered, whether in theology or in law. Dissent continued during the finest periods of Jewish history: great
scholars sharply disagreed with Maimonides; Hasidism, which
brought so much illumination and inspiration into Jewish life,
was a movement of dissent.

In the past centuries, even under conditions of repression and
of danger to their very existence, Jews continued to persist in
their dissent from both Judaism and Christianity, thus retaining
a spiritual loyalty unmatched in the history of humanity.

Judaism in its very essence came into being as an act of dissent, of dissent from paganism, as an act of nonconformity with

the surrounding culture. And unless we continue to dissent, unless we continue to say NO to idol worship in the name of a higher YES, we will revert to paganism.

The greatness of the prophets was in their ability to voice dissent and disagreements not only with the beliefs of their pagan neighbors, but also with the cherished values and habits of their *own* people.

Is there dissent in Judaism today? Creative dissent comes out of love and faith, offering positive alternatives, a vision.

The scarcity of creative dissent today may be explained by the absence of assets that make creative dissent possible: deep caring, concern, untrammeled radical thinking informed by rich learning, a degree of audacity and courage, and the power of the word. The dearth of people who are rooted in Jewish learning and who think clearly and care deeply, who are endowed with both courage and power of the word, may account for the spiritual vacuum, for the state of religious existence today.

Judaism whose stance is audacity is presented as a religion of complacency; Judaism is a call to grandeur, but what we hear is a system of trivialities, commonplace, clichés.

So much of what is given out as Jewish thinking is obsolete liberalism or narrow parochialism. The education offered in most Jewish schools in insipid, flat, and trivial.

There are dissenters in Judaism today. Yet those who attract the most attention are frivolous, while those who are authentic speak in a small still voice which the Establishment is unable to hear.   — *Unpublished manuscript*

THE SPIRIT OF JUDAISM

Religion becomes sinful when it begins to advocate the segregation of God, to forget that the true sanctuary has no walls. Religion has always suffered from the tendency to become an end in itself, to seclude the holy, to become parochial, self-indulgent, self-seeking, as if the task were not to ennoble human nature but to enhance the power and beauty of its institutions or to enlarge the body of doctrines. It has often done more to canonize prejudices than to wrestle for truth, to petrify the sacred than to sanctify the secular. Yet the task of religion is to be a challenge to the stabilization of values.   — *GSM*, 414

EXISTENCE AND CELEBRATION

Happiness is not a synonym for *self-satisfaction,* complacency, or smugness. Self-satisfaction breeds futility and despair. All that is creative in man stems from a seed of endless *discontent.* New insight begins when satisfaction comes to an end, when all that has been seen, said or done looks like a distortion.

The aim is the maintenance and fanning of a discontent with our aspirations and achievements, the maintenance and fanning of a craving that knows no satisfaction. Man's true fulfillment depends upon communication with that which transcends him.

The cure of the soul begins with a *sense of embarrassment,* embarrassment at our pettiness, prejudices, envy, and conceit; embarrassment at the profanation of life. A word that is full of grandeur has been converted into a carnival.

Man is too great to be fed upon uninspiring pedestrian ideals. We have adjusted ideals to our stature, instead of attempting to rise to the level of ideals. The ceiling of aspiration is too low: a car, color television, and life insurance. Modern man has royal power and plebeian ideals.

To the ear of a Jew who is attuned to the voice of the prophets, some of the celebrated theories of our age sound like intellectual slang. Over against all pedestrian conceptions, the Bible speaks of life in the *language of grandeur,* with a vision of sublime goals that surpasses the glamour of all empires, the summit of all theories.

Judaism is *spiritual effrontery*. The tragedy is that there is disease and starvation all over the world, and we are building more luxurious hotels in Las Vegas. Social dynamics is no substitute for moral responsibility.

The most urgent task is to destroy the myth that accumulation of wealth and the achievement of comfort are the chief vocations of man. How can adjustment to society be an inspiration to our youth if that society persists in squandering the material resources of the world on luxuries in a world where more than a billion people go to bed hungry every night? How can we speak of reverence for man and of the belief that all men are created equal without repenting the way we promote the vulgarization of existence?

What the world needs is a sense of ultimate embarrassment. Modern man has the power and the wealth to overcome poverty and disease, but he has no wisdom to overcome suspicion. We are guilty of misunderstanding the meaning of existence; we are guilty of distorting our goals and misrepresenting our souls. We are better than our assertions, more intricate, more profound than our theories maintain. *Our thinking is behind the times.* In our hands it became a platitude, adapted to the intellectual recession of the modern era. It has become an amenity of comfortable living, dividends without investment, with religious institutions — regarded as public kitchens — offering peace of mind free of charge. The demands are modest, and pretentious the rewards.

Nonchalantly we have gambled away the sublime insights of Jewish piety, the noble demands of Jewish law and observance.

This is the vocation of the few to be the witness par excellence, to insist that *man without God is a torso,* that life involves not only the satisfaction of selfish needs, but also the satisfaction of a divine need for human justice and nobility.

The Western world is a world committed to the God of Abraham. What is at stake in this grave hour of history is the right understanding of that commitment. It is no accident that, in a considerable part of the world, the Bible has been eliminated.

The tyranny of conformity tends to deprive man of his inner identity, of his ability to stand still in the midst of flux, to remain a person in the midst of a crowd. Thus the threat to modern man is loss of personhood, vanishing of identity, sinking into anonymity, not knowing who he is, whence he comes and where he goes.

Being a Jew makes anonymity impossible. A Jew represents, stands for, proclaims — even in spite of himself. The world never sees the Jew as an individual but rather as a representative of a whole tradition, of a whole people. A Jew is never alone.

Who is a Jew? A person whose integrity decays when unmoved by the knowledge of wrong done to other people.

Who is a Jew? A person in travail with God's dreams and designs, a person to whom God is a challenge, not an abstraction. He is called upon to know of God's stake in history, to be involved in the sanctification of time and in building of the Holy Land, to cultivate passion for justice and the ability to experience the arrival of Friday evening as an event.

Who is a Jew? A person who knows how to recall and to keep alive what is holy in our people's past and to cherish the promise and the vision of redemption in the days to come.

Who is a Jew? A witness to the transcendence and presence of God; a person in whose life Abraham would feel at home, a person for whom Rabbi Akiba would feel deep affinity, a person of whom the Jewish martyrs of all ages would not be ashamed.

— *MGSA*, 31–32

YOM KIPPUR

The impact of *erev* Yom Kippur was more powerful in my life than that of Yom Kippur itself. I don't know whether I can state this adequately; I find it almost impossible to convey. What really changed my life and shaped my character were the few hours before Yom Kippur. I am not going to give you a description. I can only say that they were moments in my life when

I felt somehow more than human. These were very difficult hours. It was a great challenge for us to discover whether it was still possible for us in our civilization to go through such great experiences. It was great fear and trembling, great *pahad*, great awareness that you are now to be confronted. There was no fear of punishment, not even a fear of death, but the expectation of standing in the presence of God. This was the decisive moment. Get ready; purify yourself. Terribly lacking in explicitness, but tremendously powerful. And behind it a full sense of one's own unworthiness and a sense of contrition. . . .

Let's talk about the "business" of Yom Kippur. What is it? It is the day in which God purifies us. And we will either succeed or fail with our congregations to the degree that we are able to convey precisely such a basic concept. . . . There is no *pahad* today, correct? We have no *pahad*. Everything is fine. Soon we will have helicopters in every courtyard. . . . To make the mistake we are making is to forget how much anguish there is in every human being. Scratch the skin of any person and you come upon sorrow, frustration, unhappiness. People are pretentious. Everybody looks proud; inside he is heartbroken. We have not understood how to channel this depth of human suffering into religious experience. Forgive me for saying so, but we have developed Jewish sermons as if there were no personal problems. And when we do speak about the inner problems of men we borrow from psychoanalysis, *aleha hashalom*. . . .

We are all failures. At least one day a year we should recognize it. I have failed so often. I am sure those present here have also failed. We have much to be contrite about; we have missed opportunities. The sense of inadequacy ought to be at the very center of the day.

But confessing our sins is not the only aspect of that day which we must emphasize. It is a day of great solemnity, because the day itself atones. This is the grandeur of the day, the mystery of the day. The real contrition was *erev* Yom Kippur: Yom Kippur is "good *Yontiv*."

If you don't mind, I'll tell you something my grandfather the *Oheiv Yisroel* said. We fast on both Yom Kippur and *Tisha B'av*. What is the difference between the two days? On *Tisha B'av*, he said, *ver ken essen* (who can eat)? On Yom Kippur, he said, since a Jew is like an angel, *ver darf essen* (who needs to eat)? I think that these few words offer an insight into the nature of Yom Kippur. To be angelic. It is not an empty phrase; it is a matter to be experienced and studied. One day a year we can transcend the human to enter the state of *ver darf essen*.

I would strongly advise you to stress and develop this aspect, along with the aspect of contrition. To put contrition another way, develop a sense of embarrassment. The root of any religious faith is a sense of embarrassment, of inadequacy. I would cultivate a sense of embarrassment. It would be a great calamity for humanity if the sense of embarrassment disappeared, if everybody was an all-rightnik, with an answer to every problem. We have no answer to ultimate problems. We really don't know. In this not knowing, in this sense of embarrassment, lies the key to opening the wells of creativity. Those who have no embarrassment remain sterile. We must develop this contrition or sense of embarrassment. Tell your congregation that the Book of Psalms is full of expressions of embarrassment. Teach them the meaning of sin, a word which has disappeared from the Jewish consciousness in America. We have no sin. We only have customs and ceremonies. The even more difficult, and more noble, task is transmitting the solemnity of the day. Yom Kippur is a day, *ver darf essen*. These two ideas belong to the essence of the day.   —*MGSA*, 146–47

EDUCATION

Our education seems to be concerned either with the past or with the future. We teach facts and figures, but facts are past, things that have become crystallized. We teach ideas and skills that will enable the students in their career, storing up food for the future.

We as Jews are committed to the notion that education can and must reach the inner man, that its goal is to refine and to exalt the nature of man (Genesis 17:1).

Supremely sensitive as the prophets are to the wickedness of man and deeply conscious of his stubbornness and callousness, they also insist upon the ability of man to change, to repent, to return to God and live by justice and compassion. Prophecy may be defined as a formidable effort to change any spiritual status quo, as an everlasting protest against any fatalistic conception of life, against those who teach that human nature will never change. The belief in the possibility to affect and to ennoble human beings is the rock upon which all of Judaism is built. Denial of this belief would render all of Torah innocuous. The Torah is not description but guidance; not an acceptance but a challenge; not reminiscence but commandment. It is not a portraiture of that which is, but a vision, and anticipation of that which *ought* to be.

The teacher is a witness, not only the agent of the school board. He has a mission, not just a job. The school is a intellectual sanctuary. We must wage a battle against complacency and callousness, against the worship of power and the idolatry of success. There is a battle to be waged for the restoration of man, for the revival of reverence. Sinai has not solved the ultimate problem vicariously. Sinai is the question, the Call, and it is upon us to give the answer again and again. The irrational forces within man seem to be in the majority. Reason is in the minority. To become a powerful voice it is in need of allies. Such an ally is the sense of inadequacy, the power of love and compassion, the grandeur and authority of a divine commandment. Knowledge of God has two ingredients: thought and feeling. Thought without feeling is deaf, feeling without thought is blind.   — *Unpublished manuscript*

RABBIS

What is it that American rabbis could offer the Jews of Israel?

The Jews of Israel have a profound concern for the survival of the Jews in the Diaspora. And the basic problem today is not *shlilat ha-galut,* but *shlilat ha-ruah,* negation of the spirit.

Religion in contemporary society has become an impersonal affair, an institutional loyalty. It survives on the level of activities rather than in the stillness of commitment. It has fallen victim to the belief that real is only that which is capable of being registered by fact-finding surveys.

Inwardness is ignored. The spirit has become a myth. Man treats himself as if he were created in the likeness of a machine rather than the likeness of God. The body is his god, and its needs are its prophets. Having lost his awareness of his sacred image, he became deaf to the command: to live in a way which is compatible with his image.

Judaism, too, has become an impersonal affair. By Judaism is meant what is done publicly rather than that which comes about in privacy. The chief virtue is social affiliation rather than conviction. Engaged as we were in building institutions and calling for affiliation, we have neglected to deal with the personal, the private, the intimate.

Judaism without a soul is as viable as a man without a heart. Social dynamics is no substitute for meaning. Yet, the failure to realize the fallacy of such substitution seems to be common in our days.

The soul is ignored. Man treats himself as if he were created in the likeness of a machine rather than the likeness of God. His major concern is rockets in space. His form of worship is organization. Instead of examining premises, he is making surveys.

Perhaps this is the most urgent task: to save the inner man from oblivion. To remind the world of the reality of the inner life, of the splendor of thought, of the delights of meditation, of the dignity of wonder and reverence. It is in this area that we Jews may be able to make a contribution to the world.

Perhaps this is the most urgent task: to save the inner man from oblivion, to remind ourselves that we are a duality of mysterious grandeur and pompous dust. Our future depends upon our appreciation of the reality of the inner life, of the splendor of thought, of the dignity of wonder and reverence. This is the most important thought: God has a stake in the life of a man, of every man. But this idea cannot be imposed from without; it must be discovered by every man. It cannot be preached, it must be experienced.

The congregations and national organizations push the rabbi into the role of public relations man, while the real task of the rabbi is to be a private relations man.

Our greatest mistake is to underestimate the spiritual power of the rabbi. Sermons may be forgotten, but the love, the reverence, the dedication of the rabbi affects the souls of his community and remains alive long after the rabbi has left this world.

The chief difficulty is that a layman who enters a synagogue will make no effort. He expects the rabbi to give him everything — inspiration, instruction, excitement. Unless a person knows how to pray alone, he is incapable of praying within the congregation. The future of congregational prayer depends on whether the Jews will learn how to pray when they are alone.

As a person committed to *halakha,* I say to you that *halakha* is not the central issue of this generation. The central problem is emptiness in the heart, the decreased sensitivity to the imponderable quality of the spirit, the collapse of communication between the realm of tradition and the inner world of the individual. The central problem is that we do not know how to pray, or how to cry, or how to resist the deceptions of the silent persuaders. There is no community of those who worry about integrity. Everyone of us lives in isolation.

Let us go out to those who have gone astray and teach them to distinguish between the upper and the lower levels of life. Many people delight in their wealth and wit; let us delight in reciting Psalms as said by David and the afflicted and martyred

Jews of all times. Let us adore the pioneers of prayer in an age of paganism and cruelty. Let us remember those who would never utter a lie, those who would always share their scanty meals with strangers. Let us follow those who kept the company of God in this world of misery, who welcomed angels to their homes on Friday evenings.   — *Unpublished manuscript*

NO RELIGION IS AN ISLAND

This essay was originally delivered as the inaugural lecture for the Harry Emerson Fosdick Visiting Professorship at Union Theological Seminary, which my father held during the academic year 1965–66. He delivered the lecture the evening of November 10, 1965, and referred in his speech to the widespread electrical power failure in New York City that had occurred the night before.

I speak as a member of a congregation whose founder was Abraham, and the name of my rabbi is Moses.

I speak as a person who was able to leave Warsaw, the city in which I was born, just six weeks before the disaster began. My destination was New York; it would have been Auschwitz or Treblinka. I am a brand plucked from the fire in which my people were burned to death. I am a brand plucked from the fire of an altar of Satan on which millions of human lives were exterminated to evil's greater glory and on which so much else was consumed: the divine image of so many human beings, many people's faith in the God of justice and compassion, and much of the secret and power of attachment to the Bible bred and cherished in the hearts of men for nearly two thousand years.

I speak as a person who is often afraid and terribly alarmed lest God has turned away from us in disgust and even deprived us of the power to understand His word. In the words Isaiah perceived in his vision (6:4–10):

Then I said, "Here I am! Send me." And he said, "Go, and say to this people: Hear and hear, but do not understand; see and see, but do not perceive. Make the heart of this people fat, and their ears heavy, and shut their eyes; lest they see with their eyes, and hear with their ears, and understand with their hearts, and turn and be healed."

Some of us are like patients in the state of final agony — who scream in delirium: The doctor is dead, the doctor is dead.

I speak as a person who is convinced that the fate of the Jewish people and the fate of the Hebrew Bible are intertwined. The recognition of our status as Jews, the legitimacy of our survival, is possible only in a world in which the God of Abraham is revered.

Nazism in its very roots was a rebellion against the Bible, against the God of Abraham. Realizing that it was Christianity that implanted attachment to the God of Abraham and involvement with the Hebrew Bible in the hearts of Western man, Nazism resolved that it must both exterminate the Jews and eliminate Christianity, and bring about instead a revival of Teutonic paganism.

Nazism has suffered a defeat, but the process of eliminating the Bible from the consciousness of the Western world goes on. It is on the issue of saving the radiance of the Hebrew Bible in the minds of man that Jews and Christians are called upon to work together. *None of us can do it alone.* Both of us must realize that in our age anti-Semitism is anti-Christianity and that anti-Christianity is anti-Semitism.

Man is never as open to fellowship as he is in moments of misery and distress. The people of New York City have never experienced such fellowship, such awareness of being one as they did last night in the midst of darkness.

Indeed, there is a light in the midst of the darkness of this hour. But, alas, most of us have no eyes.

Is Judaism, is Christianity, ready to face the challenge? When I speak about the radiance of the Bible in the minds of man,

I do not mean its being a theme for *Information, Please* but rather an openness to God's *presence in the Bible,* the continuous ongoing effort for a breakthrough in the soul of man, the guarding of the precarious position of being human, even a little higher than human, despite defiance and in face of despair.

The supreme issue is today not the *halakha* for the Jew or the church for the Christian — but the premise underlying both religions, namely, whether there is a *pathos,* a divine reality concerned with the destiny of man which mysteriously impinges upon history; the supreme issue is whether we are alive or dead to the challenge and the expectation of the living God. The crisis engulfs all of us. The misery and fear of alienation from God make Jew and Christian cry together.

Jews must realize that the spokesmen of the Enlightenment who attacked Christianity were no less negative in their attitude toward Judaism. They often blamed Judaism for the misdeeds of the daughter religion. The casualties of the devastation caused by the continuous onslaughts on biblical religion in modern times are to be found among Jews as well as among Christians.

On the other hand, the community of Israel must always be mindful of the mystery of aloneness and uniqueness of its own being. "There is a people that dwells apart, not reckoned among the nations" (Numbers 23:19), says the Gentile prophet Balaam. Is it not safer for us to remain in isolation and to refrain from sharing perplexities and certainties with Christians?

Our era marks the end of complacency, the end of evasion, the end of self-reliance. Jews and Christians share the perils and the fears; we stand on the brink of the abyss together. Interdependence of political and economic conditions all over the world is a basic fact of our situation. Disorder in a small obscure country in any part of the world evokes anxiety in people all over the world.

Parochialism has become untenable. There was a time when you could not pry out of a Boston man that the Boston state house is not the hub of the solar system or that one's own denomination has not the monopoly of the Holy Spirit. Today we know that even the solar system is not the hub of the universe.

The religions of the world are no more self-sufficient, no more independent, no more isolated than individuals or nations. Energies, experiences, and ideas that come to life outside the boundaries of a particular religion or all religions continue to challenge and to affect every religion.

Horizons are wider, dangers are greater.... *No religion is an island*. We are all involved with one another. Spiritual betrayal on the part of one of us affects the faith of all of us. Views adopted in one community have an impact on other communities. Today religious isolationism is a myth. For all the profound differences in perspective and substance, Judaism is sooner or later affected by the intellectual, moral, and spiritual events within the Christian society, and vice versa.

We fail to realize that while different exponents of faith in the world of religion continue to be wary of the ecumenical movement, there is another ecumenical movement, worldwide in extent and influence: nihilism. We must choose between interfaith and internihilism. Cynicism is not parochial. Should religions insist upon the illusion of complete isolation? Should we refuse to be on speaking terms with one another and hope for each other's failure? Or should we pray for each other's health and help one another in preserving one's respective legacy, in preserving a common legacy?

The Jewish Diaspora today, almost completely to be found in the Western world, is certainly not immune to the spiritual climate and the state of religious faith in the general society. We do not live in isolation, and the way in which non-Jews either relate or bid defiance to God has a profound impact on the minds and souls of the Jews. Even in the Middle Ages, when most Jews lived in relative isolation, such impact was acknowledged. To quote: "The usage of the Jews is in accordance with that of the non-Jews. If the non-Jews of a certain town are moral, the Jews born there will be so as well." Rabbi Joseph

Yaabez, a victim of the Spanish Inquisition, in the midst of the Inquisition was able to say that "the Christians believe in Creation, the excellence of the patriarchs, revelation, retribution and resurrection. Blessed is the Lord, God of Israel, who left this remnant after the destruction of the Temple. But for these Christian nations we might ourselves become infirm in our faith."

We are heirs to a long history of mutual contempt among religions and religious denominations, of religious coercion, strife, and persecutions. Even in periods of peace, the relationship that obtains between representatives of different religions is not just reciprocity of ignorance; it is an abyss, a source of detraction and distrust, casting suspicion and undoing efforts of many an honest and noble expression of good will.

The psalmist's great joy is in proclaiming: "Truth and mercy have met together" (Psalm 85:11). Yet frequently faith and the lack of mercy enter a union, out of which bigotry is born, the presumption that my faith, my motivation, is pure and holy, while the faith of those who differ in creed — even in my own community — is impure and unholy. How can we be cured of bigotry, presumption, and the foolishness of believing that we have been triumphant while we have all been defeated?

Is it not clear that in spite of fundamental disagreements there is a convergence of some of our commitments, some of our views, tasks we have in common, evils we must fight together, goals we share, a predicament afflicting us all?

On what basis do we people of different religious commitments meet one another?

First and foremost, we meet as human beings who have much in common: a heart, a face, a voice, the presence of a soul, fears, hope, the ability to trust, a capacity for compassion and understanding, the kinship of being human. My first task in every encounter is to comprehend the personhood of the human being I face, to sense the kinship of being human, solidarity of being.

To meet a human being is a major challenge to mind and heart. I must recall what I normally forget. A person is not just a specimen of the species called *Homo sapiens*. He is all of humanity in one, and whenever one man is hurt, we are all injured. The human is a disclosure of the divine, and all men are in one God's care for man. Many things on earth are precious, some are holy, humanity is holy of holies.

To meet a human being is an opportunity to sense the image of God, the *presence* of God. According to a rabbinical interpretation, the Lord said to Moses: "Wherever you see the trace of man there I stand before you...."

When engaged in a conversation with a person of different religious commitment, if I discover that we disagree in matters sacred to us, does the image of God I face disappear? Does God cease to stand before me? Does the difference in commitment destroy the kinship of being human? Does the fact that we differ in our conceptions of God cancel what we have in common: the image of God?

> For this reason was man created single (whereas of every other species many were created)...that there should be peace among human beings: one cannot say to his neighbor, my ancestor was nobler than thine (*Sanhedrin* 37a).

The primary aim of these reflections is to inquire how a Jew out of his commitment and a Christian out of his commitment can find a religious basis for communication and cooperation on matters relevant to their moral and spiritual concern in spite of disagreement.

There are four dimensions of religious existence, four necessary components of man's relationships to God: (*a*) the teaching, the essentials of which are summarized in the form of a creed, which serve as guiding principles in our thinking about matters temporal or eternal, the dimension of the doctrine; (*b*) faith, inwardness, the direction of one's heart, the intimacy of religion, the dimension of privacy; (*c*) the law, or the sacred act to be carried out in the sanctuary in society or at home, the dimension of the deed; (*d*) the context in which creed, faith, and ritual come to pass, such as the community or the covenant, history, tradition, the dimension of transcendence.

In the dimension of faith, the encounter proceeds in terms of personal witness and example, sharing insights, confessing inadequacy. On the level of doctrine we seek to convey the content of what we believe in; on the level of faith we experience in one another the presence of a person radiant with reflections of a greater presence.

I suggest that the most significant basis for meeting of men of different religious traditions is the level of fear and trembling, of humility and contrition, where our individual moments of faith are mere waves in the endless ocean of mankind's reaching out for God, where all formulations and articulations appear as understatements, where our souls are swept away by the awareness of the urgency of answering God's commandment, while stripped of pretension and conceit we sense the tragic insufficiency of human faith.

What divides us? What unites us? We disagree in law and creed, in commitments which lie at the very heart of our religious existence. We say no to one another in some doctrines essential and sacred to us. What unites us? Our being accountable to God, our being objects of God's concern, precious in His eyes. Our conceptions of what ails us may be different, but the anxiety is the same. The language, the imagination, the concretization of our hopes are different, but the embarrassment is the same, and so is the sigh, the sorrow, and the necessity to obey.

We may disagree about the ways of achieving fear and trembling, but the fear and trembling are the same. The demands are different, but the conscience is the same, and so is arrogance, iniquity. The proclamations are different, the callousness is the same, and so is the challenge we face in many moments of spiritual agony.

Above all, while dogmas and forms of worship are divergent, God is the same. What unites us? A commitment to the Hebrew

Bible as Holy Scripture. Faith in the Creator, the God of Abraham; commitment to many of His commandments, to justice and mercy; a sense of contrition; sensitivity to the sanctity of life and to the involvement of God in history; the conviction that without the holy the good will be defeated; prayer that history may not end before the end of days; and so much more.

There are moments when we all stand together and see our faces in the mirror: the anguish of humanity and its helplessness; the perplexity of the individual and the need of divine guidance; being called to praise and to do what is required.

In conversations with Protestant and Catholic theologians I have more than once come upon an attitude of condescension to Judaism, a sort of pity for those who have not yet seen the light; tolerance instead of reverence. On the other hand, I cannot forget that when Paul Tillich, Gustave Weigel, and I were invited by the Ford Foundation to speak from the same platform on the religious situation in America, we not only found ourselves in deep accord in disclosing what ails us but, above all, without prior consultation, the three of us confessed that our guides in this critical age are the prophets of Israel, not Aristotle, not Karl Marx, but Amos and Isaiah.

The theme of these reflections is not a doctrine or an institution called Christianity but human beings all over the world, both present and past, who worship God as followers of Jesus, and my problem is how I should relate myself to them spiritually. The issue I am called upon to respond to is not the truth of dogma but the faith and the spiritual power of the commitment of Christians. In facing the claim and the dogma of the church, Jews and Christians are strangers and stand in disagreement with one another. Yet there are levels of existence where Jews and Christians meet as sons and brothers. "Alas, in heaven's name, are we not your brothers, are we not the sons of one father and are we not the sons of one mother?"

To be sure, all men are sons of one father, but they have also the power to forfeit their birthright, to turn rebels, voluntary bastards, "children with no faithfulness in them" (Deuteronomy

32:20). It is not flesh and blood but honor and obedience that save the right of sonship. We claim brotherhood by being subject to His commandments. We are sons when we hearken to the Father, and we praise and honor Him.

The recognition that we are sons in obeying God and praising Him is the starting point of my reflection. "I am a companion of all who fear Thee, of those who keep Thy precepts" (Psalm 119:63). I rejoice wherever his name is praised, His presence sensed, His commandment done.

The first and most important prerequisite of interfaith is faith. It is only out of the depth of involvement in the unending drama that began with Abraham that we can help one another toward an understanding of our situation. Interfaith must come out of depth, not out of a void absence of faith. It is not an enterprise for those who are half learned or spiritually immature. If it is not to lead to the confusion of the many, it must remain a prerogative of the few.

Faith and the power of insight and devotion can only grow in privacy. Exposing one's inner life may engender the danger of desecration, distortion, and confusion. Syncretism is a perpetual possibility. Moreover, at a time of paucity of faith, interfaith may become a substitute for faith, suppressing authenticity for the sake of compromise. In a world of community, religions can easily be leveled down to the lowest common denominator.

Both communication and separation are necessary. We must preserve our individuality as well as foster care for one another, reverence, understanding, cooperation. In the world of economics, science, and technology, cooperation exists and continues to grow. Even political states, though different in culture and competing with one another, maintain diplomatic relations and strive for coexistence. Only religions are not on speaking terms. Over a hundred countries are willing to be part of the United Nations; yet no religion is ready to be part of a movement for United Religions. Or should I say, not yet ready? Ignorance, distrust, and disdain often characterize their relations to one another. Is disdain for the opposition indigenous to the religious position? Granted that Judaism and Christianity are committed to contradictory claims, is it impossible to carry on a controversy without acrimony, criticism without loss of respect, disagreement without disrespect? The problem to be faced is how to combine loyalty to one's own tradition with reverence for different tradition. How is mutual esteem between Christian and Jew possible?

A Christian ought to ponder seriously the tremendous implications of a process begun in early Christian history. I mean the conscious or unconscious de-Judaization of Christianity, affecting the church's way of thinking, its inner life as well as its relationship to the past and present reality of Israel — the father and mother of the very being of Christianity. The children did not arise to call the mother blessed; instead they called the mother blind. Some theologians continue to act as if they did not know the meaning of "Honor your father and mother"; others, anxious to prove the superiority of the church, speak as if they suffered from a spiritual Oedipus complex.

A Christian ought to realize that a world without Israel would be a world without the God of Israel. A Jew, on the other hand, ought to acknowledge the eminent role and part of Christianity in God's design for the redemption of all men.

Modern Jews who have come out of the state of political seclusion and are involved in the historic process of Western mankind cannot afford to be indifferent to the religious situation of our fellow men. Opposition to Christianity must be challenged by the question: What religious alternative do we envisage for the Christian world? Did we not refrain for almost two thousand years from preaching Judaism to the nations?

A Jew ought to ponder seriously the responsibility involved in Jewish history for having been the mother of two religions. Does not the failure of children reflect upon their mother? Do not the sharp deviations from Jewish tradition on the part of early Christians who were Jewish indicate some failure of communication within the spiritual climate of the first-century Palestine?

Judaism is the mother of the Christian faith. It has a stake in the destiny of Christianity. Should a mother ignore her child, even a wayward, rebellious one? On the other hand, the church should acknowledge that we Jews, in loyalty to our tradition, have a stake in its faith, recognizing our vocation to preserve and to teach the legacy of the Hebrew Scriptures and accept our aid in fighting anti-Marcionite trends as an act of love.

Is it our duty to help one another in trying to overcome hardening of heart, in cultivating a sense of wonder and mystery, in unlocking doors to holiness in time, in opening minds to the challenge of the Hebrew Bible, in seeking to respond to the voice of the prophets?

No honest religious person can fail to admire the outpouring of the love of man and the love of God, the marvels of worship, the magnificence of spiritual insight, the piety, charity, and sanctity in the lives of countless men and women, manifested in the history of Christianity. Have not Pascal, Kierkegaard, Immanuel Kant, and Reinhold Niebuhr been a source of inspiration to many Jews?

Over and above mutual respect we must acknowledge indebtedness to one another. It is our duty to remember that it was the church that brought the knowledge of the God of Abraham to the Gentiles. It was the church that made Hebrew Scripture available to mankind. This we Jews must acknowledge with a grateful heart.

The Septuagint, the works of Philo, Josephus, as well as the Apocrypha and Pseudepigrapha, the *Fons vitae* by Ibn Cabirol would have been lost had they not been preserved in monasteries. Credit for major achievements in modern scholarship in the field of Bible, in biblical as well as Hellenistic Jewish history, goes primarily to Protestant scholars.

The purpose of religious communication among human beings of different commitments is mutual enrichment and enhancement of respect and appreciation rather than the hope that the person spoken to will prove to be wrong in what he regards as sacred.

Dialogue must not degenerate into a dispute, into an effort on the part of each to get the upper hand. There is an unfortunate history of Christian-Jewish disputations, motivated by the desire to prove how blind the Jews are and carried on in a spirit of opposition, which eventually degenerated into enmity. Thus a conversation between Christian and Jew in which abandonment of the partner's faith is a silent hope must be regarded as offensive to one's religious and human dignity.

Let there by an end to disputation and polemic, an end to disparagement. We honestly and profoundly disagree in matters of creed and dogma. Indeed, there is a deep chasm between Christians and Jews concerning, e.g., the divinity and messiahship of Jesus. But across the chasm we can extend our hands to one another.

Religion is a means, not an end. It becomes idolatrous when regarded as an end in itself. Over and above all being stands the Creator and Lord of history, He who transcends all. To equate religion and God is idolatry.

Does not the all-inclusiveness of God contradict the exclusiveness of any particular religion? The prospect of all men embracing one form of religion remains an eschatological hope. What about here and now? Is it not blasphemous to say: I alone have all the truth and the grace, and all those who differ live in darkness and are abandoned by the grace of God?

Is it really our desire to build a monolithic society: one party, one view, one leader, and no opposition? Is religious uniformity desirable or even possible? Has it really proved to be a blessing for a country when all its citizens belonged to one denomination? Or has any denomination attained a spiritual climax when it had the adherence of the entire population? Does not the task of preparing the Kingdom of God require a diversity of talents, a variety of rituals, soul-searching as well as opposition?

Perhaps it is the will of God that in this eon there should be diversity in our forms of devotion and commitment to Him. In this eon diversity of religions is the will of god.

In the story of the building of the Tower of Babel we read: "The Lord said: They are one people, and they have all one language, and this is what they begin to do" (Genesis 11:6). These words are interpreted by an ancient rabbi to mean: What has caused them to rebel against me? The fact that they are one people and they have all one language....

> For from the rising of the sun to its setting my name is great among the nations, and in every place incense is offered to my name and a pure offering; for my name is great among the nations, says the Lord of hosts. (Malachi 1:11)

This statement refers undoubtedly to the contemporaries of the prophet. But who were these worshipers of one God? At the time of Malachi there were hardly a large number of proselytes. Yet the statement declares: All those who worship their gods do not know it, but they are really worshiping me.

It seems that the prophet proclaims that men all over the world, though they confess different conceptions of God, are really worshiping one God, the father of all men, though they may not be aware of it.

Religions, I repeat, true to their own convictions, disagree profoundly and are in opposition to one another on matters of doctrine. However, if we accept the prophet's thesis that they all worship one God, even without knowing it, if we accept the principle that the majesty of God transcends the dignity of religion, should we not regard a divergent religion as His Majesty's loyal opposition? However, does not every religion maintain the claim to be true, and is not truth exclusive?

The ultimate truth is not capable of being fully and adequately expressed in concepts and words. The ultimate truth is about the situation that pertains between God and man. "The Torah speaks in the language of man." Revelation is always an accommodation to the capacity of man. No two minds are alike, just as not two faces are alike. The voice of God reaches the spirit of man in a variety of ways, in a multiplicity of languages. One truth comes to expression in many ways of understanding.

A major factor in our religious predicament is due to self-righteousness and to the assumption that faith is found only in him who has arrived, while it is absent in him who is on the way. Religion is often inherently guilty of the sin of pride and presumption. To paraphrase the prophet's words, the exultant religion dwelt secure and said in her heart: "I am, and there is no one besides me."

Humility and contrition seem to be absent where most required — in theology. But humility is the beginning and end of religious thinking, the secret test of faith. There is no truth without humility, no certainty without contrition.

Ezra the Scribe, the great renovator of Judaism, of whom the rabbis said that he was worthy of receiving the Torah had it not been already given through Moses, confessed his lack of perfect faith. He tells us that after he had received a royal *firman* from King Artaxerxes granting him permission to lead a group of exiles from Babylonia: "I proclaimed a fast there at the river Ahava, that we might afflict ourselves before our God, to seek of Him a right way for us, and for our little ones, and for all substance. For I was ashamed to require of the king a band of soldiers and horsemen to help us against the enemy in the way: because we had spoken unto the king, saying, The hand of God is upon all them for good that seek Him" (8:21–22).

Human faith is never final, never an arrival, but rather an endless pilgrimage, a being on the way. We have no answers to all problems. Even some of our sacred answers are both emphatic and qualified, final and tentative; final within our own position in history, tentative because we can speak only in the tentative language of man.

Heresy is often a roundabout expression of faith, and sojourning in the wilderness is a preparation for entering the Promised Land.

Is the failure, the impotence of all religions, due exclusively to human transgression? Or perhaps to the mystery of God's withholding His grace, of His concealing even while revealing? Disclosing the fulness of His glory would be an impact that would surpass the power of human endurance.

His thoughts are not our thoughts. Whatever is revealed is abundance compared with our soul and a pittance compared with His treasures. No word is God's last word, no word is God's ultimate word.

Following the revelation at Sinai, the people said to Moses: "You speak to us, and we will hear; let not God speak to us, lest we die" (Exodus 20:19).

The Torah as given to Moses, an ancient rabbi maintains, is but an unripened fruit of the heavenly tree of wisdom. At the end of days, much that is concealed will be revealed.

The mission to the Jews is a call to the individual Jew to betray the fellowship, the dignity, the sacred history of his people. Very few Christians seem to comprehend what is morally and spiritually involved in supporting such activities. We are Jews as we are men. The alternative to our existence as Jews is spiritual suicide, extinction. It is not a change into something else. Judaism has allies but no substitutes.

The wonder of Israel, the marvel of Jewish existence, the survival of holiness in the history of the Jews is a continuous verification of the marvel of the Bible. Revelation to Israel continues as a revelation throughout Israel.

The Protestant pastor Christian Furchtegott Gellert was asked by Frederick the Great, "Herr Professor, give me proof of the Bible, but briefly, for I have little time." Gellert answered, "Your Majesty, the Jews."

Indeed, is not the existence of the Jews a witness to the God of Abraham? Is not our loyalty to the Law of Moses a light that continues to illuminate the lives of those who observe it as well as the lives of those who are aware of it?

Gustave Weigel spent the last evening of his life in my study at the Jewish Theological Seminary. We opened our hearts to one another in prayer and contrition and spoke of our own deficiencies, failures, hopes. At one moment I posed the question: Is it really the will of God that there be no more Judaism in the world? Would it really be the triumph of God if the scrolls of the Torah were no longer taken out of the Ark and the Torah no longer read in the synagogue, our ancient Hebrew prayers in which Jesus himself worshiped no more recited, the Passover Seder no longer celebrated in our lives, the Law of Moses no longer observed in our homes? Would it really be *ad majorem Dei gloriam* to have a world without Jews?

My life is shaped by many loyalties — to my family, to my friends, to my people, to the U.S. Constitution, etc. Each of my loyalties has its ultimate root in one ultimate relationship: loyalty to God, the loyalty of all my loyalties. That relationship is the Covenant of Sinai. All we are we owe to Him. He has enriched us with gifts and insight, with the joy of moments full of blessing. He has also suffered with us in years of agony and distress.

None of us pretends to be God's accountant, and His design for history and redemption remains a mystery before which we must stand in awe. It is as arrogant to maintain that the Jews' refusal to accept Jesus as the Messiah is due to their stubbornness or blindness as it would be presumptuous for the Jews not to acknowledge the glory and holiness in the lives of countless Christians. "The Lord is near to all who call upon Him, to all who call upon Him in truth" (Psalm 145:18).

Fortunately there are some important Christian voices who expressed themselves to the effect that the missionary activities to the Jews be given up. Reinhold Niebuhr may have been the first Christian theologian who, at a joint meeting of the faculties of the Union Theological Seminary, and the Jewish Theological Seminary declared that

> the missionary activities are wrong not only because they are futile and have little fruit to boast for their exertions. They are wrong because the two faiths despite differences are sufficiently alike for the Jew to find God more easily in terms of his own religious heritage than by subjecting himself to the hazards of guilt feelings involved

in conversion to a faith which, whatever its excellencies, must appear to him as a symbol of an oppressive majority culture.... Practically nothing can purify the symbol of Christ as the image of God in the imagination of the Jew from the taint with which ages of Christian oppression in the name of Christ have tainted it.

Paul Tillich has said,

> Many Christians feel that it is a questionable thing, for instance, to try to convert Jews. They have lived and spoken with their Jewish friends for decades. The have not converted them, but they have created a community of conversation which has changed both sides of the dialogue.

And a statement on "relations with the Roman Catholic Church" adopted by the Central Committee of the World Council of Churches, in its meeting in Rochester, New York, in August 1963, mentions proselytism as a "cause of offence," an issue "which must be frankly faced if true dialogue is to be possible."

The ancient rabbis proclaimed: "Pious men of all nations have a share in the life to come."

"I call heaven and earth to witness that the Holy Spirit rests upon each person, Jew or Gentile, man or woman, master or slave, in consonance with his deeds."

Holiness is not the monopoly of any particular religion or tradition. Wherever a deed is done in accordance with the will of God, wherever a thought of man is directed toward Him, there is the holy.

The Jews do not maintain that the way of the Torah is the only way of serving God. "Let all the peoples walk each one in the name of its god, but we will walk in the name of the Lord our God for ever and ever" (Micah 4:5).

"God loves the Saint" (Psalm 146:8) — "They love Me, and I love them.... If a person wishes to be a Levite or a priest, he cannot become a saint, even if he is a Gentile, he may become one. For saints do not derive their saintliness from the ancestry; they become saints because they dedicate themselves to God and love Him." Conversion to Judaism is no prerequisite for sanctity. In his Code Maimonides asserts:

> Not only is the tribe of Levi (God's portion) sanctified in the highest degree, but any man among all the dwellers on earth whose heart prompts him and whose mind instructs him to dedicate himself to the services of God and to walk uprightly as God intended him to, and who disencumbers himself of the load of the many pursuits which men invent for themselves.
>
> God asks for the heart, everything depends upon the intention of the heart ... all men have a share in eternal life if they attain according to their ability knowledge of the Creator and have ennobled themselves by noble qualities. There is no doubt that he who has thus trained himself morally and intellectually to acquire faith in the Creator will certainly have a share in the life to come. This is why our rabbis taught: A Gentile who studies the Torah of Moses is (spiritually) equal to the High Priest at the Temple in Jerusalem.

Leading Jewish authorities, such as Yehudah Halevi and Maimonides, acknowledge Christianity to be *preparatio messianica,* while the church regarded ancient Judaism to have been a *preparatio evangelica.* Thus, whereas Christian doctrine has often regarded Judaism as having outlived its usefulness and the Jews as candidates for conversion, the Jewish attitude enables us to acknowledge the presence of a divine plan in the role of Christianity within the history of redemption. Yehudah Halevi, though criticizing Christianity and Islam for retaining relics of ancient idolatry and feast days — "They also revere places sacred to idols" — compares Christians and Mohammedans to proselytes who adopted the roots but not all the branches (or the logical conclusions of the divine commandments).

The wise providence of God towards Israel may be compared to the planting of a seed of corn. It is placed in
the earth, where it seems to be changed into soil, and
water, and rottenness, and the seed can no long be recognized. But in very truth it is the seed that has changed
the earth and water into its own nature, and then the
seed raises itself from one stage to another, transforms
the elements, and throws out shoots and leaves.... Thus
it is with the Christians and Muslims. The Law of Moses
has changed them that come into contact with it, even
though they seem to have cast the Law aside. These religions are the preparation and the preface to the Messiah
we expect, who is the fruit himself of the seed originally
sown, and all men, too, will be fruit of God's seed when
they acknowledge Him, and all become one mighty tree.

A similar view is set forth by Maimonides in his authorita-
tive Code:

It is beyond the human mind to fathom the designs of the
Creator; for our ways are not His ways, neither are our
thoughts His thoughts. All these matters relating to Jesus
of Nazareth and the Ishmaelite (Mohammed) who came
after him served to clear the way for King Messiah, to prepare the whole world to worship God with one accord,
as it is written, "For then will I turn to the peoples a pure
language, that they may all call upon the name of the Lord
to serve Him with one consent" (Zephaniah 3:9). Thus
the messianic hope, the Torah, and the commandments
have become familiar topics — of conversation (among the
inhabitants) of the far isles and many peoples....

Christianity and Islam, far from being accidents of history
or purely human phenomena, are regarded as part of God's
design for the redemption of all men. Christianity is accorded
ultimate significance by acknowledging that "all these matters
relating to Jesus of Nazareth and [Mohammed]...served to

clear the way for King Messiah." In addition to the role of these religions in the plan of redemption, their achievements within history are explicitly affirmed. Through them "the messianic hope, the Torah, and the commandments have become familiar topics...(among the inhabitants) of the far isles and many peoples." Elsewhere Maimonides acknowledges that "the Christians believe and profess that the Torah is God's revelation (*torah min ha-shamayim*) and given to Moses in the form in which it has been preserved; they have it completely written down, though they frequently interpret it differently."

Rabbi Johanan Ha-Sandelar, a disciple of Rabbi Akiba, says: "Every community which is established for the sake of heaven will in the end endure, but one which is not for the sake of heaven will not endure in the end."

Rabbi Jacob Emden maintains the heretical Jewish sects such as the Karaites and the Sabbatians belong to the second category, whereas Christianity and Islam are in the category of "a community which is for the sake of heaven" and which will "in the end endure." They have emerged out of Judaism and accepted "the fundamentals of our divine religion...to make known God among the nations...to proclaim that there is a Master in heaven and earth, divine providence, reward and punishment....Who bestows the gift of prophecy...and communicates through the prophets laws and statutes to live by.... This is why their community endures.... Since their intention is for the sake of heaven, reward will not be withheld from them." He also praises many Christian scholars who have come to the rescue of Jews in their literature.

Rabbi Israel Lifschutz of Danzig (1782–1860) speaks of the Christians, "our brethren, the Gentiles, who acknowledge the one God and revere His Torah which they deem divine and observe, as is required by them, the seven commandments of Noah...."

What, then, is the purpose of interreligious cooperation?

It is neither to flatter nor to refute one another, but to help one another; to share insight and learning, to cooperate in academic ventures on the highest scholarly level and, what is even more important, to search in the wilderness for wellsprings of devotion, for treasures of stillness, for the power of love and care for men. What is urgently needed are ways of helping one another in the terrible predicament of here and now by the courage to believe that the word of the Lord endures forever as well as here and now; to cooperate in trying to bring about a resurrection of sensitivity, a revival of conscience; to keep alive the divine sparks in our souls, to nurture openness to the spirit of the Psalms, reverence for the words of the prophets, and faithfulness to the Living God.   —*MGSA,* 235–50

5

Prayer Makes Us Worthy of Being Saved

My father wrote extensively about prayer, including a book, Man's Quest for God, *published in 1954. With all of his magnificent evocation of the experience of prayer, he never spoke in first-person terms about his own experiences, preferring to maintain the privacy necessary for the intimacy of prayer. To pray, for him, was not only a verbal experience, but an inward transformation and a transformation of the world around him. A mitzvah, he writes, is a prayer in the form of a deed. When he returned from the Voting Rights march led by Martin Luther King Jr. in Selma, Alabama, in 1965, he said, "I felt my legs were praying."*

How can we understand an experience as intimate and private as prayer? How can those who have never prayed, nor feel they are able to pray, understand prayer? Is prayer ultimately unintelligible — only a personal experience, not something that can be translated into words and analyzed?

Theodor Adorno, the German-Jewish philosopher, raised a similar question about art: "Aesthetics cannot hope to grasp works of art if it treats them as hermeneutical objects. What at present needs to be grasped is their unintelligibility.... Achieving an adequate interpretive understanding of a work of art

means demystifying certain enigmatic dimensions without trying to shed light on its constitutive enigma.... To solve a riddle
in art is to identify the reason why it is insoluble — which is
the gaze artworks direct at the viewer."* Prayer lies in that
same realm: it cannot be easily grasped, interpreted, laid bare,
or conveyed to others. It is an enigma, unintelligible, perhaps,
but profoundly powerful. A story my father used to tell is about
someone who gazes through a window at people jumping and
moving and thinks they are mad. Then he goes inside and hears
the music: they are dancing. From the outside, prayer and religious observance are difficult to understand. Only when the
inner music is perceived can the religious expression begin to
have meaning.

The Sabbath, too, can be prayer in the form of a day. The
Sabbath is a day of rest and also a day of rejoicing. How
we sanctify, how we celebrate, how we create holiness out of
time — that is the question and the central task given to Jews.
These are tasks that are difficult to carry out alone, but require
inspiration and guidance from others. Music was always the
central aesthetic for my father, and his paean to the role of the
cantor in the synagogue, bringing music as a tool of sanctification, expresses the intimacy he saw between prayer and music.
His words on sermons, by contrast, are an injunction to the
rabbis, not an accolade.

His criticisms of synagogue services were abundant and un-
restrained. He had no patience for synagogues that had been
transformed into social networks of suburban Jews, nor for
Jews for whom halakha had become ritual and custom and
prayer a performance by the rabbi and cantor. If God was not
present, it was not prayer. The hope for the future of Judaism
in America, he would say, lies with the black church. There is
where he found the kind of religiosity that reminded him of his
Hasidic environment growing up in Warsaw.

---

*Theodor Adorno, *Aesthetic Theory* (London: Routledge, 1984), 173, 177, 179.

THE ABILITY TO ANSWER

We do not refuse to pray. We merely feel that our tongues are tied, our minds inert, our inner vision dim, when we are about to enter the door that leads to prayer. We do not refuse to pray; we abstain from it. We ring the hollow bell of selfishness rather than absorb the stillness that surrounds the world, hovering over all the restlessness and fear of life — the secret stillness that precedes our birth and succeeds our death. Futile self-indulgence brings us out of tune with the gentle song of nature's waiting, of mankind's striving for salvation. Is not listening to the pulse of wonder worth silence and abstinence from self-assertion? Why do we not set apart an hour of living for devotion to God by surrendering to stillness? We dwell on the edge of mystery and ignore it, wasting our souls, risking our stake in God. We constantly pour our inner light away from Him, setting up the thick screen of self between Him and us, adding more shadows to the darkness that already hovers between Him and our wayward reason. Accepting surmises as dogmas and prejudices as solutions, we ridicule the evidence of life for what is more than life. Our mind has ceased to be sensitive to the wonder. Deprived of the power of devotion to what is more important than our individual fate, steeped in passionate anxiety to survive, we lose sight of what fate is, of what living is. Rushing through the ecstasies of ambition, we only awake when plunged into dread or grief. In darkness, then, we grope for solace, for meaning, for prayer.

But there is a wider voluntary entrance to prayer than sorrow and despair — the opening of our thoughts to God. We cannot make Him visible to us, but we can make ourselves visible to Him. So we open our thoughts to Him — feeble our tongues, but sensitive our hearts. We see more than we can say. The trees stand like guards of the Everlasting; the flowers like signposts of His goodness — only *we* have failed to be testimonies to His presence, tokens of His trust. How could we have lived in the shadow of greatness and defied it?

Mindfulness of God rises slowly, a thought at a time. Suddenly we are there. Or is He here, at the margin or our soul? When we begin to feel a qualm of difference lest we hurt what is holy, lest we break what is whole, then we discover that He is not austere. He answers with love our trembling awe. Repentant of forgetting Him even for a while, we become sharers of gentle joy; we would like to dedicate ourselves forever to the unfoldment of His final order.

To pray is to take notice of the wonder, to regain a sense of the mystery that animates all beings, the divine margin in all attainments. Prayer is *our* humble *answer* to the inconceivable surprise of living. It is all we can offer in return for the mystery by which we live. Who is worthy to be present at the constant unfolding of time? Amidst the meditation of mountains, the humility of flowers — wiser than all alphabets — clouds that die constantly for the sake of His glory, we are hating, hunting, hurting. Suddenly we feel ashamed of our clashes and complaints in the face of the tacit glory in nature. It is so embarrassing to live! How strange we are in the world, and how presumptuous our doings! Only one response can maintain us: gratefulness for witnessing the wonder, for the gift of our unearned right to serve, to adore, and to fulfill. It is gratefulness which makes the soul great.

However, we often lack the strength to be grateful, the courage to answer, the ability to pray. To escape from the mean and penurious, from calculating and scheming, is at times the parching desire of man. Tired of discord, he longs to escape from his own mind — and for the peace of prayer. How good it is to wrap oneself in prayer, spinning a deep softness of gratitude to God around all thoughts, enveloping oneself in the silken veil of song! But how can man draw song out of his heart if his consciousness is a woeful turmoil of fear and ambition? He has nothing to offer but disgust, and the weariness of wasting the soul. Accustomed to winding strands of thoughts, to twisting phrases in order to be successful, he is incapable of finding simple, straight words. His language abounds in traps and decoys, in shams and tricks, in gibes and sneers. In the teeth of such powerful distractions, he has to focus all the powers of his mind on one concern. In the midst of universal agitation, how can there be tranquility?

Trembling in the realization that we are a blend of modesty and insolence, of self-denial and bias, we beseech God for rescue, for help in the control of our thoughts, words, and deeds. We lay all our forces before Him. Prayer is arrival at the border. The dominion is Thine. Take away from me all that may not enter Thy realm.

As a tree torn from the soil, as a river separated from its source, the human soul wanes when detached from what is greater than itself. Without the holy, the good turns chaotic; without the good, beauty become accidental. It is the patter of the impeccable which makes the average possible. It is the attachment to what is spiritually superior: loyalty to a sacred person or idea, devotion to a noble friend or teacher, love for a people or for mankind, which holds our inner life together. But any ideal, human, social, or artistic, if it forms a roof over all of life, shuts us off from the light. Even the palm of one hand may bar the light of the entire sun. Indeed, we must be open to the remote in order to perceive the near. Unless we aspire to the utmost, we shrink to inferiority.

Prayer is our attachment of the utmost. Without God in sight, we are like the scattered rungs of a broken ladder. To pray is to become a ladder on which thoughts mount to God to join the movement toward Him which surges unnoticed throughout the entire universe. We do not step out of the world when we pray; we merely see the world in a different setting. The self is not the hub, but the spoke of the revolving wheel. In prayer we shift the center of living from self-consciousness to self-surrender. God is the center toward which all forces tend. He is the source, and we are the flowing of His force, the ebb and flow of His tides.

Prayer takes the mind out of the narrowness of self-interest and enables us to see the world in the mirror of the holy. For when we betake ourselves to the extreme opposite of the ego, we can behold a situation from the aspect of God. Prayer is a way to master what is inferior in us, to discern between the signal and the trivial, between the vital and the futile, by taking counsel with what we know about the will of God, by seeing our fate in proportion to God. Prayer clarifies our hope and intentions. It helps us discover our true aspirations, the pangs we ignore, the longings we forget. It is an act of self-purification, a quarantine for the soul. It gives us the opportunity to be honest, to say what we believe, and to stand for what we say. For the accord of assertion and conviction, of thought and conscience, is the basis of all prayer.

Prayer teaches us what to aspire to. So often we do not know what to cling to. Prayer implants in us the ideals we ought to cherish. Redemption, purity of mind and tongue, or willingness to help may hover as ideas before our mind, but the idea becomes a concern, something to long for, a goal to be reached, when we pray: "Guard my tongue from evil and my lips from speaking guile; and in the face of those who curse me, let my soul be silent" [from the daily liturgy].

Prayer is the essence of spiritual living. Its spell is present in every spiritual experience. Its drive enables us to delve into what is what beneath our beliefs and desires and to emerge with a renewed taste for the infinite simplicity of the good. On the globe of the microcosm the flow of prayer is like the Gulf Stream, imparting warmth to all that is cold, melting all that is hard in our life. For even loyalties may freeze to indifference if detached from the stream which carries the strength to be loyal. How often does justice lapse into cruelty, and righteousness into hypocrisy. Prayer revives and keeps alive the rare greatness of some past experience in which things glowed with meaning and blessing. It remains important, even when we ignore it for awhile, like a candlestick set aside for the day. Night will come, and we shall again gather round its tiny flame. Our affection for the trifles of living will be mixed with longing for the comfort of all men.

However, prayer is no panacea, no substitute for action. It is, rather, like a beam thrown from a flashlight before us into the darkness. It is in this light that we who grope, stumble, and climb discover where we stand, what surrounds us, and the course which we should choose. Prayer makes visible the right and reveals what is hampering and false. In its radiance, we behold the worth of our efforts, the range of our hopes, and the meaning of our deeds. Envy and fear, despair and resentment, anguish and grief, which lie heavily upon the heart, are dispelled like shadows by its light.

Sometimes prayer is more than a light before us; it is a light within us. Those who have once been resplendent with this light find little meaning in speculations about the efficacy of prayer. A story is told about a rabbi who once entered heaven in a dream. He was permitted to approach the temple of Paradise where the great sages of the Talmud, the Tannaim, were spending their eternal lives. He saw that they were just sitting around tables studying the Talmud. The disappointed rabbi wondered, "Is this all there is to Paradise?" But suddenly he heard a voice, "You are mistaken. The Tannaim are not in Paradise. Paradise is in the Tannaim." —*MQG*, 4–8

ON PRAYER: YOUNG PEOPLE

Many young people suffer from a fear of the self. They do not feel at home in their own selves. The inner life is a place of dereliction, a no man's land, inconsolate, weird. The self has become a place from which to flee. The use of narcotic drugs is a search for a home.

Human distress — wretchedness, agony — is a signal of a universal distress. It is a sign of human misery; it also proclaims a divine predicament. God's mercy is too great to permit the innocent to suffer. But there are forces that interfere with God's mercy, with God's power. This is a dreadful mystery as well as a challenge: God is held in captivity.

I pray because God, the *Shekhinah,* is an outcast. I pray
because God is in exile, because we all conspire to blur all signs
of His presence in the present or in the past. I pray because
I refuse to despair, because extreme denials and defiance are
refuted in the confrontation of my own presumption and the
mystery all around me. *I pray because I am unable to pray.*

And suddenly I am forced to do what I seem unable to do.
Even callousness to the mystery is not immortal. There are
moments when the clamor of all sirens dies, presumption is
depleted, and even the bricks in the walls are waiting for a song.
The door is closed, the key is lost. Yet the new sadness of my
soul is about to open the door.

Some souls are born with a scar, others are endowed with
anesthesia. Satisfaction with the world is base and the ultimate
callousness. The remedy for absurdity is still to be revealed. The
irreconcilable opposites which agonize human existence are the
outcry, the prayer. Every one of us is a cantor; every one of
us is called to intone a song, to put into prayer the anguish
of all.

God is in captivity in this world, the oblivion of our lives.
God is in search of man, in search of a home in the soul and
deeds of man. God is not at home in our world. Our task is
to hallow time, to enable Him to enter our moments, to be at
home in our time, in what we do with time.

Ultimately, prayer in Judaism is an act in the messianic
drama. We utter the words of the *Kaddish: Magnified and sanc-
tified be His great name in the world which He has created
according to His will.* Our hope is to enact, to make real the
magnification and sanctification of this name here and now.

There is a pressing urgency to the work of justice and compassion. As long as there is a shred of hatred in a human heart,
as long as there is a vacuum without compassion anywhere in
the world, there is an emergency.

Why do people rage? People rage and hurt and do not know
how to regret, how to repent. The problem is not that people
have doubts but rather that people may not even care to doubt.

The charity we may do is terribly diminutive compared with what is required. You and I have prayed, have craved to be able to make gentleness a certainty, and have so often failed. But there are in the world so many eyes streaming with tears, hearts dumb with fears, that to be discouraged would be treason.

The predicament of prayer is twofold: not only do we not know how to pray; we do not know what to pray for.

We have lost the ability to be shocked.

The malignity of our situation is increasing rapidly, the magnitude of evil is spreading furiously, surpassing our ability to be shocked. The human soul is too limited to experience dismay in proportion to what has happened in Auschwitz, in Hiroshima.

We do not know what to pray for. Should we not pray for the ability to be shocked at atrocities committed by man, for the capacity to be dismayed at our inability to be dismayed?

Prayer should be an act of catharsis, of purgation of emotions, as well as a process of self-clarification, of examining priorities, of elucidating responsibility. Prayer not verified by conduct is an act of desecration and blasphemy. Do not take a word of prayer in vain. Our deeds must not be a refutation of our prayers.

It is with shame and anguish that I recall that it was possible for a Roman Catholic church adjoining the extermination camp in Auschwitz to offer communion to the officers of the camp, to people who day after day drove thousands of people to be killed in the gas chambers.

Let there be an end to the separation of church and God, of sacrament and callousness, of religion and justice, of prayer and compassion.

A home is more than an exclusive habitat, mine and never yours. A residence devoid of hospitality is a den or a hole, not a home. Prayer must never be a citadel for selfish concerns but rather a place for deepening concern over other people's plight. Prayer is a privilege. Unless we learn how to be worthy, we forfeit the right and ability to pray.

Prayer is meaningless unless it is subversive, unless it seeks to overthrow and to ruin the pyramids of callousness, hatred, opportunism, falsehoods.   — *MGSA*, 260, 262

BEYOND FAITH

To have no faith is callousness; to have undiscerning faith is superstition. "The simple believeth every word" (Proverbs 14:15), frittering away his faith on things explorable but not yet explored. By confounding ignorance with faith he is inclined to regard as exalted whatever he fails to understand, as if faith began where understanding ended, as if it were a supreme virtue to be convinced without proofs, to be ready to believe.

Faith, the soul's urge to rise above its own wisdom, to be, like a plant, a little higher than the soil, is irrepressible, often frantic, wayward, blind, and exposed to peril. The soul's affinity for the holy is strong enough to outwit or to repress but not annihilate the force of gravitation to the vile. Those who are sure of their faith often tumble under their own weight, and, when overthrown, they fall on their knees, worshiping, deifying the snake that usually lies where flowers grow. How much tender devotion, heroism, and self-mortification have been lavished upon the devil? How often has man deified Satan, found the evil magnificent though dismal and full of indescribable majesty? Faith is, indeed, no security.

It is tragically true that we are often wrong about God, believing in that which is not God, in a counterfeit ideal, in a dream, in a cosmic force, in our own father, in our own selves. We must never cease to question our own faith and to ask what God means to us. Is He an alibi for ignorance? The white flag of surrender to the unknown? Is He a pretext for comfort and unwarranted cheer? A device to cheat despondency, fear or despair?

From whom should we seek support for our faith if even religion can be fraud, if by self-sacrifice we may hallow murder?

From our minds, which have so often betrayed us? From our conscience, which easily fumbles and fails? From the heart? From our good intentions? "He that trusteth in his own heart is a fool" (Proverbs 28:26).

> The heart is deceitful about all things,
> It is exceedingly weak —
> Who can know it.
>   (Jeremiah 17:9)

Individual faith is not self-sufficient: it must be countersigned by the dictate of unforgettable guidance.

Significantly, the Shema, the main confession of Jewish faith, is not written in the first person and does not express a personal attitude: I believe. All it does is to recall the Voice that said: "Hear, O Israel."

Not the individual man, nor a single generation by its own power can erect the bridge that leads to God. Faith is the achievement of ages, an effort accumulated over centuries. Many of its ideas are as the light of a star that left its source centuries ago. Many songs, unfathomable today, are the resonance of voices of bygone times. There is a collective memory of God in the human spirit, and it is this memory of which we partake in our faith.

It has been suggested that the group-memory of acquired characteristics is an important factor in man's development. Some of our a priori categories are collective in character and lacking in individual content. They acquire individual character through the encounter with empirical facts. "In a sense they must be deposits from the experiences of the ancestors" [C. G. Jung].

The heritage of mankind includes not only dispositions but also ideas, "motives and images which can spring anew in every age and clime, without tradition or migration" [C. G. Jung]. "The true story of the mind is not preserved in learned volumes, but in the living mental organism of everyone." There is a treasure house in our group memory. "Nothing has been lost except the key to this treasure-house, and even that is occasionally found."

The riches of a soul are stored up in its memory. This is the test of character — not whether a man follows the daily fashion, but whether the past is alive in his present. When we want to understand ourselves, to find out what is most precious in our lives, we search our memory. Memory is the soul's witness to the capricious mind.

Only those who are spiritually imitators, only people who are afraid to be grateful and too weak to be loyal, have nothing but the present moment. To a noble person it is a holy joy to remember, an overwhelming thrill to be grateful; while to a person whose character is neither rich nor strong, gratitude is a most painful sensation. The secret of wisdom is never to get lost in a momentary mood or passion, never to forget friendship because of a momentary grievance, never to lose sight of the lasting values because of a transitory episode. The things which sweep through our daily life should be valued according to whether or not they enrich the inner cistern. That only is valuable in our experience which is worth remembering. Remembrance is the touchstone of all actions.

Memory is a source of faith. To have faith is to remember. Jewish faith is a recollection of that which happened to Israel in the past. The events in which the spirit of God became a reality stand before our eyes painted in colors that never fade. Much of what the Bible demands can be comprised in one word: *Remember.* "Take heed to thyself, and keep thy soul diligently lest thou forget the things which thine eyes saw, and lest they depart from thy heart all the days of thy life; make them known unto thy children and thy children's children" (Deuteronomy 4:9).

Jews have not preserved the ancient monuments; they have retained the ancient moments. The light kindled in their history was never extinguished. With sustaining vitality the past survives in their thoughts, hearts, rituals. Recollection is a holy act: we sanctify the present by remembering the past.

It is perhaps for this reason that we find in some of the Jewish prayer books two summaries of the Jewish doctrine, one, based on the teaching of Maimonides, contains the famous thirteen tenets, and the other a list of remembrances. It is as if the essential things in Judaism were not abstract ideas but rather concrete events. The exodus from Egypt, the giving of the Torah on Mount Sinai, the destruction of the Temple of Jerusalem had to be constantly present in the mind of a Jew. For over eighteen centuries the people have been away from the Holy Land, and still their attachment to the Land of Israel has never been severed. The soul of Israel has pledged: "If I forget thee, O Jerusalem, may my right hand forget its cunning" (Psalm 137:5).

Not far off from our consciousness there is a slow and silent stream, a stream not of oblivion but of memory, from which souls must constantly drink before entering the realm of faith. When drinking from that stream we do not have to take a leap in order to reach the level of faith. What we must do is to be open to the stream in order to echo, in order to recall.

— MNA, 159–63

OUT OF THE DEPTH WE CRY FOR HELP

Out of the depth we cry for help. We believe that we are able to overcome ulterior motives, since otherwise no good would be done, and no love would be possible. Yet "to attain purity of heart we are in need of divine help." This is why we pray:

> Purify our hearts so that we may worship Thee in honesty.
> (The Sabbath Liturgy)

All is inadequate: our actions as well as our abstentions. We cannot rely on our devotion, for it is tainted with alien thoughts, conceit, and vanity. It requires a great effort to *realize before Whom we stand,* for such realization is more than having a thought in one's mind. It is a knowledge in which the whole person in involved; the mind, the heart, body, and soul. To know it is to forget everything else, including the self. At best, we can only attain it for an instant, and only from time to time.

What then is left for us to do except *to pray for the ability to pray*, to bewail our ignorance of living in His presence? And even if such prayer is tainted with vanity, His mercy accepts and redeems our feeble efforts. It is the continuity of trying to pray, the unbroken loyalty to our duty to pray, that lends strength to our fragile worship; and it is the holiness of the community that bestows meaning upon our individual acts of worship. These are the three pillars on which our prayer rises to God: our own loyalty, the holiness of Israel, the mercy of God.

— GSM, 407–8

THE SABBATH

To set apart one day a week for freedom, a day on which we would not use the instruments which have been so easily turned into weapons of destruction, a day for being with ourselves, a day of detachment from the vulgar, of independence of external obligations, a day on which we stop worshiping the idols of technical civilization, a day on which we use no money, a day of armistice in the economic struggle with our fellow men and the forces of nature — is there any institution that holds out a greater hope for man's progress than the Sabbath?

The solution of mankind's most vexing problem will not be found in renouncing technical civilization, but in attaining some degree of independence of it.

In regard to external gifts, to outward possessions, there is only one proper attitude — to have them and not be able to do without them. On the Sabbath we live, as it were, *independent of technical civilization*: we abstain primarily from any activity that aims at remaking or reshaping the things of space.

Man's royal privilege to conquer nature is suspended on the seventh day.

What are the kinds of labor not to be done on the Sabbath? They are, according to the ancient rabbis, all those acts which were necessary for the construction and furnishing of the Sanctuary in the desert. The Sabbath itself is a sanctuary which we build, *a sanctuary in time.*

It is one thing to race or be driven by the vicissitudes that menace life, and another thing to stand still and to embrace the presence of an eternal moment.

The seventh day is the armistice in man's cruel struggle for existence, a truce in all conflicts, personal and social, peace between man and man, man and nature, peace within man; a day on which handling money is considered a desecration, on which man avows his independence of that which is the world's chief idol. The seventh day is the exodus from tension, the liberation of man from his own muddiness, the installation of man as a sovereign in the world of time.

In the tempestuous ocean of time and toil there are islands of stillness where man may enter a harbor and reclaim his dignity. The island is the seventh day, the Sabbath, a day of detachment from things, instruments, and practical affairs as well as of attachment to the spirit.

The Sabbath must all be spent "in charm, grace, peace, and great love . . . for on it even the wicked in hell find peace." It is, therefore, a double sin to show anger on the Sabbath. "Ye shall kindle no fire throughout your habitations on the Sabbath day" (Exodus 35:3) is interpreted to mean: "Ye shall kindle no fire of controversy nor the heat of anger." Ye shall kindle no fire — not even the fire of righteous indignation.

Out of the days through which we fight and from whose ugliness we ache, we look to the Sabbath as our homeland, as our source and destination. It is a day in which we abandon our plebeian pursuits and reclaim our authentic state, in which we may partake of a blessedness in which we are what we are, regardless of whether we are learned or not, of whether our career is a success or a failure; it is a day of independence of social conditions.

All week we may ponder and worry whether we are rich or poor, whether we succeed or fail in our occupations, whether we accomplish or fall short of reaching our goals. But who could feel distressed when gazing at spectral glimpses of eternity, except to feel startled at the vanity of being so distressed?

The Sabbath is no time for personal anxiety or care, for any activity that might dampen the spirit of joy. The Sabbath is no time to remember sins, to confess, to repent, or even to pray for relief or anything we might need. It is a day for praise, not a day for petitions. Fasting, mourning, demonstrations of grief are forbidden. The period of mourning is interrupted by the Sabbath. And if one visits the sick on the Sabbath; one should say: "It is the Sabbath, one must not complain; you will soon be cured." One must abstain from toil and strain on the seventh day, even from strain in the service of God.

Why are the Eighteen Benedictions not recited on the Sabbath? It is because the Sabbath was given to us by God for joy, for delight, for rest, and should not be marred by worry or grief. Should there be a sick one in the household, we might remember this while reciting the benediction: "Heal the sick," and would become saddened and gloomy on the Sabbath day. It is for this same reason that we recite in the Sabbath grace after meals the request that "there be no sadness or trouble in the day of our rest." It is a sin to be sad on the Sabbath day.

For the Sabbath is a day of harmony and peace, peace between man and within man, and peace with all things. On the seventh day man has no right to tamper with God's world, to change the state of physical things. It is a day of rest for *man and animal* alike:

> In it thou shalt not do any manner of work, thou nor thy son, nor thy daughter, nor thy man-servant, nor thy maid-servant, nor thine *ox*, nor thine *ass*, nor any of thy *cattle*, nor thy stranger that is within thy gates, that thy man-servant and thy maid-servant may rest as well as thou.

Rabbi Solomon of Radomsk once arrived in a certain town, where, he was told, lived an old woman who had known the famous Rabbi Elimelech. She was too old to go out, so he went to see her and asked her to tell him what she knew about the great Master. [She replied:]

> I do not know what went on in his room, because I worked as one of the maids in the kitchen of his house. Only one thing I can tell you. During the week the maids would often quarrel with one another, as is common. But, week after week, on Friday when the Sabbath was about to arrive, the spirit in the kitchen was like the spirit on the eve of the Day of Atonement. Everybody would be overcome with an urge to ask forgiveness of each other. We were all seized by a feeling of affection and inner peace.

The Sabbath, thus, is more than an armistice, more than an interlude; it is a profound conscious harmony of man and the world, a sympathy for all things and a participation in the spirit that unites what is below and what is above. All that is divine in the world is brought into union with God. This is Sabbath, and the true happiness of the universe.

"Six days shalt thou labor and do all thy work (Exodus 20:8). Is it possible for a human being to do all his work in six days? Does not our work always remain incomplete? What the verse means to convey is: Rest on the Sabbath as if all your work were done. Another interpretation: *Rest even from the thought of labor.*"

A pious man once took a stroll in his vineyard on the Sabbath. He saw a breach in the fence, and then determined to mend it when the Sabbath would be over. At the expiration of the Sabbath he decided: since the thought of repairing the fence occurred to me on the Sabbath I shall never repair it.

But the Sabbath as experienced by man cannot survive in exile, a lonely stranger among days of profanity. It needs the companionship of all other days. All days of the week must be spiritually consistent with the Day of Days. All our life should

be a pilgrimage to the seventh day; the thought and appreciation of what this day may bring to us should be ever present
in our minds. For the Sabbath is the counterpoint of living;
the melody sustained throughout all agitations and vicissitudes
which menace our conscience; our awareness of God's presence
in the world.

What *we are* depends on what *the Sabbath is* to us. The law
of the Sabbath day is in the life of the spirit what the law of
gravitation is in nature.

Nothing is as hard to suppress as the will to be a slave to
one's own pettiness. Gallantly, ceaselessly, quietly, man must fight
for inner liberty. Inner liberty depends upon being exempt from
domination of things as well as from domination of people. There
are many who have acquired a high degree of political and social
liberty, but only very few are not enslaved to things. This is our
constant problem — how to live with people and remain free,
how to live with things and remain independent.

—Sabbath, 28–32, 89

CELEBRATION

The power of being human is easily dissolved in the process of
excessive trivialization. Banality and triteness, the by-products
of repetitiveness, continue to strangle or corrode the sense of
significant being. Submerged in everydayness, man begins to
treat all hours alike. The days are drab, the nights revolt in
the helplessness of despair. All moments are stillborn, all hours
seem stale. There is neither wonder nor praise. What is left is
disenchantment, the disintegration of being human.

How should one prevent the liquidation of one's power to
experience everydayness as events? How should one ease the
pressures of diluting human being to just being-around?

Events and the sense of surprise are not only inherent in the
quintessence of reality and authentic consciousness; they are the

points from which misunderstandings of human existence proceed. The question is not where is the event and what is the surprise, but how to see through the sham of routine, how to refute the falsehood of familiarity. Boredom is a spiritual disease, infectious and deadening, but curable.

The self is always in danger of being submerged in anonymity, of becoming a thing. To celebrate is to contemplate the singularity of the moment and to enhance the singularity of the self. What was shall not be again.

The biblical words about the genesis of heaven and earth are not words of information but words of appreciation. The story of creation is not a description of how the world came into being but a song about the glory of the world's having come into being. "And God saw that it was good" (Genesis 1:25). This is the challenge: to reconcile God's view with our experience.

We, however, live on borrowed notions, rely on past perceptions, thrive on inertia, delight in relaxation. Insight is a strain, we shun it frequently or even permanently. The demand, as understood in biblical religion, is to be alert and open to what is happening. What is, happens, comes about. Every moment is a new arrival, a new bestowal. How to welcome the moment? How to respond to the marvel?

The cardinal sin is in our failure not to sense the grandeur of the moment, the marvel and mystery of being, the possibility of quiet exaltation.

The secret of spiritual living is the power to praise. Praise is the harvest of love. Praise precedes faith. First we sing; then we believe. The fundamental issue is not faith but sensitivity and praise, being ready for faith.

To be overtaken with awe of God is not to entertain a feeling but to share in a spirit that permeates all being. "They all thank, they all praise, they all say: There is no one like God." As an act of personal recognition our praise would be fatuous; it is meaningful only as an act of joining in the endless song.

We praise with the pebbles on the road which are like petrified amazement, with all the flowers and trees which look as if
hypnotized in silent devotion.

To be human involves the ability to appreciate as well
as the ability to give expression to appreciation. For thousands of years authentic existence included both manipulation
and appreciation, utilization and celebration, both work and
worship. In primitive society they were interdependent; in biblical religion they were interrelated. Today we face a different
situation.

Man may forfeit his sense of the ineffable. To be alive is
a commonplace; the sense of radical amazement is gone; the
world is familiar, and familiarity does not breed exaltation
or even appreciation. Deprived of the ability to praise, modern man is forced to look for entertainment; entertainment is
becoming compulsory.

The man of our time is losing the power of celebration. Instead
of celebrating, he seeks to be amused or entertained. Celebration
is an active state, an act of expressing reverence or appreciation. To be entertained is a passive state: it is to receive pleasure
afforded by an amusing act or a spectacle. Entertainment is a
diversion, a distraction of the attention of the mind from the
preoccupations of daily living. Celebration is a confrontation,
giving attention to the transcendent meaning of one's actions.

Celebration is an act of expressing respect or reverence for
that which one needs or honors. In modern usage, the term sug-
gests demonstrations, often public demonstrations, of joy and
festivity, such as singing, shouting, speechmaking, feasting, and
the like. Yet what I mean is not outward ceremony and public
demonstration, but rather inward appreciation, lending spiritual form to everyday acts. Its essence is to call attention to the
sublime or solemn aspects of living, to rise above the confines
of consumption.

To celebrate is to share in a greater joy, to participate in an
eternal drama. In acts of consumption the intention is to please

our own selves; in acts of celebration the intention is to extol God, the spirit, the source of blessing.

What is the purpose of knowledge? We are conditioned to believe that the purpose of knowledge is to utilize the world. We forget that the purpose of knowledge is also to celebrate God. God is both present and absent. To celebrate is to invoke His presence concealed in His absence.

The mind is in search of rational coherence, the soul in quest of celebration. Knowledge is celebration. Truth is more than equation of thing and thought. Truth transcends and unites both thing and thought. Truth is transcendence; its comprehension is loyalty.

To the sense of indebtedness the meaning of existence lies in reciprocity. In receiving a pleasure, we must return a prayer; in attaining a success, we radiate compassion. The world is not mere material for exploitation. We have the right to consume because we have the power to celebrate.

Since indebtedness is an essential ingredient of existence, the inability to celebrate is a sign of insolvency, of an inability to pay the existential debt. There is no celebration without earnestness, without solemnity and reverence.

We are losing the power of appreciation; we are losing the ability to sing. Celebration without appreciation is an artificial, impersonal ceremony. A renewal of our strength will depend on our ability to reopen forgotten resources.

The meaning of existence is experienced in moments of exaltation. Man must strive for the summit in order to survive on the ground. His norms must be higher than his behavior; his ends must surpass his needs. The security of existence lies in the exaltation of existence.

This is one of the rewards of being human: quiet exaltation, capability for celebration. It is expressed in a phrase which Rabbi Akiba offered to his disciples:

> A song every day.
> A song every day.

Man in quest for an anchor in ultimate meaning is far from being a person shipwrecked who dreams of a palace while napping on the edge of an abyss. He is a person in full mastery of his ship who has lost his direction because he failed to remember his destination. Man in his anxiety is a *messenger who forgot the message.*

It is an accepted fact that the Bible has given the world a new concept of God. What is not realized is the fact that the Bible has given the world a new vision of man. The bible is not a book about God; it is a book about man.

From the perspective of the Bible:

Who is man? *A being in travail with God's dreams and designs,* with God's dream of a world redeemed, of reconciliation of heaven and earth, of a mankind which is truly His image, reflecting His wisdom, justice, and compassion. God's dream is not to be alone, to have mankind as a partner in the drama of continuous creation. By whatever we do, by every act we carry out, we either advance or obstruct the drama of redemption; we either reduce or enhance the power of evil.

— *WIM,* 114–19

THE VOCATION OF THE CANTOR

What does a person expect to attain when entering a synagogue? In the pursuit of learning one goes to a library; for aesthetic enrichment one goes to the art museum; for pure music to the concert hall. What then is the purpose of going to the synagogue? Many are the facilities which help us to acquire the important worldly virtues, skill, and techniques. But where should one learn about the insights of the spirit? Many are the opportunities for public speech; where are the occasions for inner silence? It is easy to find people who will teach us how to be eloquent; but who will teach us how to be still? It is surely important to develop a sense of humor; but is it not also important to have a sense of reverence? Where should one learn the eternal wisdom of compassion? the fear of being cruel? the danger of being callous? Where should one learn that the greatest truth is found in contrition? Important and precious as the development of our intellectual faculties is, the cultivation of a sensitive conscience is indispensable. We are all in danger of sinking into the darkness of vanity; we are all involved in worshiping our own egos. Where should we become sensitive to the pitfalls of cleverness or to the realization that expediency is not the acme of wisdom?

We are constantly in need of self-purification. We are in need of experiencing moments in which the spiritual is as relevant and as concrete, for example, as the aesthetic. Everyone has a sense of beauty; everyone is capable of distinguishing between the beautiful and the ugly. But we also must learn to be sensitive to the spirit. It is in the synagogue where we must try to acquire such inwardness, such sensitivity.

To attain a degree of spiritual security one cannot rely upon one's own resources. One needs an atmosphere, where the concern for the spirit is shared by a community. We are in need of students and scholars, masters and specialists. But we need also the company of witnesses, of human beings who are engaged in worship, who for a moment sense the truth that life is meaningless without attachment to God. It is the task of the cantor to create the liturgical community, to convert a plurality of praying individuals into a unity of worship.

Pondering his religious existence a Jew will realize that some of the greatest spiritual events happen in moments of prayer. Worship is the source of religious experience, of religious insight, and religiously some of us live by what happens to us in the hours we spend in the synagogue. These hours have been in the past the wellsprings of insight, the wellsprings of faith. Are these wellsprings still open in our time?

Following a service, I overhead an elderly lady's comment to her friend, "This was a charming service!" I felt like crying. Is this what prayer means to us? God is grave; He is never charming. But we think that it is possible to be sleek and to pray,

"Serve the Lord with fear and rejoice with trembling" (Psalm 2:11). Prayer is joy and fear, trust and trembling together.

I grew up in a house of worship where the spiritual was real. There was no elegance, but there was contrition; there was no great wealth, but there was great longing. It was a place where when seeing a Jew I sensed Judaism. Something happened to the people when they entered a house of worship. To this day every time I go to the synagogue my hope is to experience a taste of such an atmosphere. But what do I find within the contemporary synagogue? We are all in agreement about the importance of prayer. Cantors dedicate their lives to the art of leading our people in prayer. Indeed, of all religious acts, prayer is the most widely observed. Every Seventh Day hundreds of thousands of Jews enter the synagogue. But what comes to pass in most of our services?

One must realize the difficulties of the cantor. The call to prayer often falls against an iron wall. The congregation is not always open and ready to worship. The cantor has to pierce the armor of indifference. He has to fight for a response. He has to conquer them in order to speak for them. Often he must first be one who awakens those who slumber, before he can claim to be a *sheliah sibbur.* And yet we must not forget that there is a heritage of spiritual responsiveness in the souls of our people. It is true, however, that this responsiveness may waste away for lack of new inspiration, just as fire burns itself out for lack of fuel.

The tragedy of the synagogue is in the depersonalization of prayer. *Hassanuth* has become a skill, a technical performance, an impersonal affair. As a result the sounds that come out of the *hassan* evoke no participation. They enter the ears; they do not touch the hearts. The right Hebrew word for cantor is *ba'al tefillah,* master of prayer. The mission of a cantor is to lead in prayer. He does not stand before the Ark as an artist in isolation, trying to demonstrate his skill or to display vocal feats. He stands before the Ark not as an individual but with a congregation. He must identify himself with the congregation. His task is to represent as well as to inspire a community. Within the synagogue music is not an end in itself but a means of religious experience. Its function is to help us to live through a moment of confrontation with the presence of God, to expose ourselves to Him in praise, in self-scrutiny, and in hope.

We have adopted the habit of believing that the world is a spiritual vacuum, whereas the seraphim proclaim that "the whole earth is full of His glory." Are only the seraphim endowed with a sense for the glory? "The heavens declare the glory of God." How do they declare it? How do they reveal it? "There is no speech, there are no words, neither is their voice hard." The heavens have no voice; the glory is inaudible. And it is the task of man to reveal what is concealed, to be the voice of the glory, to sing its silence, to utter, so to speak, what is in the heart of all things. The glory is here — invisible and silent. Man is the voice; his task to be the song. The cosmos is a congregation in need of a cantor. Every Seventh Day we proclaim as a fact.

> They all thank Thee,
> They all praise Thee,
> They all say,
> There is none holy like the Lord.

Whose ear has ever heard how all trees sing to God? Has our reason ever thought of calling upon the sun to praise the Lord? And yet, what the ear fails to perceive, what reason fails to conceive, our prayer makes clear to our souls. It is a higher truth, to be grasped by the spirit: "All Thy works shall give Thee thanks, O Lord" (Psalm 145:10).

We are not alone in our acts of praise. Wherever there is life, there is silent worship. The world is always on the verge of becoming one in adoration. It is man who is the cantor of the universe and in whose life the secret of cosmic prayer is disclosed. To sing means to sense and to affirm that the spirit is real and that its glory is present. In singing we perceive what is otherwise beyond perceiving. Song, and particularly liturgical song, is not only an act of expression but also a way of bringing down the spirit from heaven to earth. The numerical value of the letters which constitute the word *shirah*, or song, is equal to the numerical value of the word *tefillah*, or prayer. Prayer is song. Sing to Him, chant to Him, meditate about all the wonders (1 Chronicles 16:9), about the mystery that surrounds us. The wonder defies all descriptions; the mystery surpasses the limits of expression. The only language that seems to be compatible with the wonder and mystery of being is the language of music. Music is more than just expressiveness. It is rather a reaching out toward a realm that lies beyond the reach of verbal propositions. Verbal expression is in danger of being taken literally and of serving as a substitute for insight. Words become slogans; slogans become idols. But music is a refutation of human finality. Music is an antidote to higher idolatry.

While other forces in society combine to dull our mind, music endows us with moments in which the sense of the ineffable becomes alive.

Listening to great music is a shattering experience, throwing the soul into an encounter with an aspect of reality to which the mind can never relate itself adequately. Such experiences undermine conceit and complacency and may even induce a sense of contrition and a readiness for repentance. I am neither a musician nor an expert on music. But the shattering experience of music has been a challenge to my thinking on ultimate issues. I spend my life working with thoughts. And one problem that gives me no rest is: Do these thoughts ever rise to the heights reached by authentic music?...

Music leads us to the threshold of repentance, of unbearable realization of our own vanity and frailty and of the terrible relevance of God. I would define myself as a person who has been smitten by music, as a person who has never recovered from the blows of music. And yet, music is a vessel that may hold anything. It may express vulgarity; it may impart sublimity. It may utter vanity; it may inspire humility. It may engender fury; it may kindle compassion. It may convey stupidity, and it can be the voice of grandeur. It often voices man's highest reverences, but often brings to expression frightful arrogance....

A cantor who faces the holiness in the Ark rather than the curiosity of man will realize that his audience is God. He will learn to realize that his task is not to entertain but to represent the people Israel. He will be carried away into moments in which he will forget the world, ignore the congregation, and be overcome by the awareness of Him in whose presence he stands. The congregation then will hear and sense that the cantor is not giving a recital but worshiping God, that to pray does not mean to listen to a singer but to identify oneself with what is being proclaimed in their name.

Entering the synagogue, I first relinquish all I know and try to begin all over again. The words are sometimes open, and at other times locked. Even in such embarrassment song is a sphere that will admit even the poor in faith. It is so far off, and yet we are all there. Pride begins to fade bit by bit, and praise begins to happen. The cantorial voice is a door, but often the banging of the door jars and tears our sensitivity to shreds....

The *siddur* is a book which everyone talks about, but few people have really read, a book which has the distinction of being one of the least known books in our literature. Do we ever ponder the meaning of its words?...

We must learn how to study the inner life of the words that fill the world of our Prayer Book. Without intense study of their meaning, we indeed feel bewildered when we encounter the multitude of those strange, lofty beings that populate the inner cosmos of the Jewish spirit. The trouble with the Prayer Book is that it is too great for us, too lofty. Our small souls must first rise to its grandeur. We have failed to introduce our minds to its greatness, and our souls are lost in its sublime wilderness. It is not enough to know how to translate Hebrew into English; it is not enough to have met a word in the dictionary and to have experienced unpleasant adventures with it in the study of grammar. A word has a soul, and we must learn how to attain insight into its life. Words are commitments, not only the subject matter for aesthetic reflection.

This is our affliction. We say words but make no decisions. We do not even know how to look across a word to its meaning. We forget how to find the way to the word, how to be on intimate terms with a few passages in the Prayer Book. We are familiar with all words, but at home with none. The *siddur* has become a foreign language which the soul does not know how to pronounce.

In order for cantorial music to regain its dignity, it will not be enough to study the authentic pattern of our musical tradition. What is necessary is a *liturgical revival.* This will involve not only a new sense of reverence and faith, but also a new insight into the meaning of the liturgical words as well as an intimate way of uttering and appropriating the words. The decline of *hassanuth* will continue as long as we fail to realize that reverence and faith are as important as talent and technique and that the music must not lose its relationship to the spirit of the words.

It is important for the cantor to study the score, but it is also important to study the words of the Prayer Book. The education of the cantor calls for intellectual and not only aesthetic achievements. In Judaism study is a form of worship, but it may also be said that worship is in a sense a form of study; it includes meditation. It is not enough to rely on one's voice. It takes a constant effort to find a way to the grandeur of the words in the Prayer Book.

What are we exposed to in the atmosphere of the synagogue? We are exposed neither to sacred words alone, nor to spiritual tunes alone. This, indeed, is the essence of our liturgy. It is a combination of the word *and* music. Great as music is, it is neither the ultimate nor the supreme. The ultimate is God, and the medium in which His guidance has been conveyed to us in *the word.* We have no holy music; we revere sacred Scripture, sacred words. Music is the language of mystery. But there is something which is greater than mystery. God is the meaning beyond all mystery. That meaning is concealed in the biblical words, and our prayers are an attempt to disclose to ourselves what is concealed in those words.

For all its grandeur, there is something greater than music. At Sinai we hear thunder and lightning, but it was not the music of the elements but the word, for the sake of which the great event happened. The Voice goes on forever, and we are being pursued by it. We have neither icons nor statues in our synagogue. We are not even in need of visible symbols to create in us a mood of worship. All we have are words in the liturgy and reverence in our hearts. But even these two are often apart from each other. It is the task of music to bring them together.

"Who shall ascend the hill of the Lord, and who shall stand in His holy place? He who has clean hands and a pure heart, and who does not lift up his soul to what is false and does not swear deceitfully" (Psalm 24:3–4). Not by might of voice, not by strength of talent alone, but by the sense of awe and fear, by contrition and the sense of inadequacy, will a cantor succeed in leading others to prayer. The cantor must constantly learn how to be involved in what he says, realizing that he must also teach others how to attach themselves to the words of the liturgy. He has a secret mission to convert, to lead people to a point where they can sense that arrogance is an abyss and sacrifice is eternity.

There are hardly proofs for the existence of God, but there are witnesses. Foremost among them are the Bible and music. Our liturgy is a moment in which these two witnesses come to expression. "On the evidence of two witnesses a claim is sustained." Our liturgy consists of the testimony of both music and the word. Perhaps this is the way to define a *ba'al tefillah*. He is a person in whom two witnesses meet. He is a person in whom a spiritual equation takes place — the equation of song and soul, of word and mind. The self and prayer are one.

I should like to conceive *hassanuth* as the art of *siddur* exegesis, as the art of interpreting the words of the liturgy. Words die of routine. The cantor's task is to bring them to life. A cantor is a person who knows the secret of the resurrection of the words.

The art of giving life to the words of our liturgy requires not only the personal involvement of the cantor but also the power contained in the piety of the ages. Our liturgy contains incomparably more than what our hearts are ready to feel. Jewish liturgy in text and in song is a spiritual summary of our history. There is a written and an unwritten Torah, Scripture and tradition. We Jews claim that one without the other is unintelligible. In the same sense we may say that there is a *written and an unwritten liturgy*. There is the liturgy but there is also an inner approach and response to it, a way of giving life to the words, a style in which the words become a personal and unique utterance.

The Lord commanded Noah: "Go into the *tevah*, you and all your household" (Genesis 7:1). *Tevah* means ark; it also means word. In prayer a person must enter the word with all he has, with heart and soul, with thought and voice. "Make a light for the *tevah*." The word is dark. This is the task of him who prays: to kindle a light in the word. Humbly we must approach both the word and the chant. We must never forget that the word is deeper than our thought, that the song is more sublime than our voice. The words enhance us. The rabbis maintain that "those who carried the Ark were actually carried by the Ark." And indeed he who knows how to carry a word in all its splendor is carried away by the word. He who has succeeded in kindling a light within the word will discover that the word has kindled a light within his soul. Where is the *Shekhinah*? Where is the presence of God to be sensed? According to *Tikkune Zohar* the *Shekhinah* is in words; God is present in sacred words. In praying we discover the holiness in words....

Awe is the prerequisite of faith and an essential ingredient of being a cantor. The loss of awe one must feel in the presence of a congregation, unawareness of how poor we are in spirit and in deeds, is a dangerous deprivation.

A learned man lost all his sources of income and was looking for a way to earn a living. The members of his community, who admired him for his learning and piety, suggested to him to serve as their cantor on the Days of Awe. But he considered himself unworthy of serving as the messenger of the community, as the one who should bring the prayers of his fellow men to the Almighty. He went to his master, the rabbi of Husiatin, and told him of his sad plight, of the invitation to serve as a cantor in the Days of Awe, and of his being afraid to accept it and to pray for his congregation. "*Be* afraid — and pray," was the answer of the rabbi. — *IF,* 242–53

PREACH IN ORDER TO PRAY

In the light of such a decision about the preeminence of prayer, the role as well as the nature of the sermon will have to be re-examined. The prominence given to the sermon as if the sermon were the core and prayer the shell is not only a drain on the intellectual resources of the preacher but also a serious deviation from the spirit of our tradition. The sermon, unlike prayer, has never been considered as one of the supreme things in this world. If the vast amount of time and energy invested in the search of ideas and devices for preaching, if the fire spent on the altar of oratory were dedicated to the realm of prayer, we would not find it too difficult to convey to others what it means to utter a word in the presence of God.

Preaching is either an organic part of the act of prayer or out of place. Sermons indistinguishable in spirit from editorials in the *New York Times,* urging us to have faith in the *New Deal, the Big Three,* or *the United Nations,* or attempting to instruct us in the latest theories of psychoanalysis, will hardly inspire us to go on to the *musaf* (the last part of the service) and to vow,

> Through all generations
> we will declare Thy greatness;
> To all eternity
> we will proclaim Thy holiness;

Thy praise, our God,
shall never depart from our mouth.

Preach in order to pray. Preach in order to inspire others to pray. The test of a true sermon is that it can be converted to prayer.

To the average worshiper many texts of perennial significance have become vapid and seem to be an assembly line of syllables. It is, therefore, a praiseworthy custom for the rabbi to bring forth the meaning of the prayers to the congregation. Unfortunately, some rabbis seem to think that their task is to teach popular science, and as a result some services are conducted as if they were *adult-education* programs. Dwelling on the historical aspects, they discuss, for example, the date of composition of the prayers, the peculiarities of their literary form, or the supposedly primitive origin of some of our laws and customs.

What about the spirit of prayer? What about relating the people to the truth of its ideas? Too often, so-called explanation kills inspiration. The suggestion that the Day of Atonement grew out of a pagan festival is, regardless of its scientific merit, hardly consonant with the spirit of *Kol Nidre* (the evening service of the Day of Atonement).

Nor must prayer be treated as an ancestral institution. In explaining sections of the Prayer Book, our task is not to give a discourse about quaint customs or about "the way our fathers used to think." The liturgy is not a museum of intellectual antiquities, and the synagogue is not a house of lectureship but a house of worship. The purpose of such comments is to inspire "outpouring of the heart" rather than to satisfy historical curiosity, to set forth the hidden relevance of ideas rather than hypotheses about forgotten origins.   —*MQG*, 79–81

6

God Is of No Importance Unless He Is of Supreme Importance

My father only rarely wrote about his life, and when he did, he emphasized his childhood years, growing up in Warsaw in a Hasidic family: the teachings he learned and, most important, the religious atmosphere he absorbed. He tells us, in his Introduction to A Passion for Truth, *that he was immersed as a child in the teachings of his Hasidic ancestors. The most important of these was the rebbe after whom he was named, Abraham Joshua Heschel, known as "the Apter Rav" and often called the "ohev Yisrael," the lover of Israel, which is the title of his one book. The Apter Rav was asked to come to Mezbizh, the village in Ukraine where the Hasidic movement's founder, the Baal Shem Tov (Besht), had lived. There the Apter Rav restored the personal, charismatic dimension of Hasidism, in contrast to its more theoretical and intellectual promoters. The Apter tradition was about love, gentleness, nourishing the soul, overcoming depression and sadness. The Apter Rav insisted that we serve God in joy and that sadness be removed from our souls, especially on the Sabbath, which he viewed as a day for the soul to rise to great heights. Individuals have obligations, he taught, because God is like the sun: He can spoil or nourish, depending upon how well we prepare ourselves. And the task of the rebbe is to help his followers prepare themselves.*

As a rebbe, he was known for his great compassion, and the stories told about him remind me of my father, who used to tell me those stories. One day the rebbe's assistant asked him how he could possibly remember all the hundreds of people who came to him, poured out their troubles, and asked him to pray for them. When someone pours out their troubles to me, he replied, it makes a scar on my heart. When I come to pray, I take out my heart and I say, look God, at all these scars. That was, in fact, precisely how my father would listen to me — and, I am sure, to the many others who poured out their hearts to him. In the tradition of his great ancestor, he opened his heart and our troubles made scars.

At the age of nine, my father writes, the presence of another Hasidic rebbe, Menachem Mendel of Kotzk, entered his life with very different kinds of teachings. The Kotzker tradition was sharp, relentless, austere, and not at all steeped in compassion. His emphasis was on truth, justice, integrity. Rather than mercy and love, he emphasized God as a judge who makes demands. His critical disdain for the spurious pieties of "religious" people was similar to that of the Danish Lutheran theologian Søren Kierkegaard, my father claimed.

There are several underlying agendas to my father's discussion of the two Hasidic approaches. He explains that both live inside of him: his heart was with the Besht and his mind was in Kotzk. The tension between them can be seen in nearly all of my father's writings: the gentle way he speaks of awe, on the one hand, and the severe way he insists that a pious person can never say, I am a good person. Such tensions between loving compassion and radical demands for truth mark the inner lives of many religious people, who find it difficult at times to keep the two in balance. At the same time, my father speaks of the Kotzker as a voice for our day, with his "haunting awareness of the terrible danger of human cruelty." Imagine such a person: "the Holocaust would not have come as a surprise to his soul." In his horror over the pretense of religiosity and his inability to remain tranquil in the face of mendacity, the Kotzker gave voice to much of what my father experienced in his struggles against the war in Vietnam and in opposing the racism of white Americans. It is the Kotzker's spirit, my father writes, that speaks to the post-Auschwitz era.

How do the religious leaders of Hasidism compare to the scholars of religion whom my father encountered at the University of Berlin, where he studied from 1927 to 1933? In a semi-autobiographical text that is also a parable with wide applicability, my father describes how he came as a pious Jew to learn about religion from German professors. Which side better understood the Bible and the inner life of religious people? What the professors failed to realize is that religion is not a manifestation of human social organization, psychological weakness, or aesthetic pleasure. Rather, it is "God's desire that I pray. . . . God's will that I believe."

Man is not alone because God is unwilling to be alone. God is not an idea intended to serve our needs, and not an explanation, a comfort, or a support. Rather, we are a "concern of God." And for us, "God is of no importance unless He is of supreme importance." Our lives, he concludes, are gifts from God, and the deepest wisdom is to repay that gift with service to other human beings.

WHY I HAD
TO WRITE THIS BOOK

I was born in Warsaw, Poland, but my cradle stood in Mesbizh (a small town in the province of Podolia, Ukraine), where the Baal Shem Tov, founder of the Hasidic movement, lived during the last twenty years of his life. That is where my father came from, and he continued to regard it as his home. He confided in me, "For I was indeed stolen out of the land of the Hebrews" (Genesis 40:15). It was because of the advice of his spiritual mentor, Reb David Moshe, his uncle, the rebbe of Tshortokov, son of Reb Israel of Rizhin, that he took up residence in Poland.

I was named after my grandfather, Reb Abraham Joshua Heschel — "the Apter Rav," and last great rebbe of Mezbizh. He was marvelous in all his ways, and it was as if the Baal Shem Tov had come to life in him. When he died in 1825, he was buried next to the holy Baal Shem. The Apter Rav claimed that his soul had lived in several incarnations, and for his descendants it was as if he had never died.

Enchanted by a wealth of traditions and tales, I felt truly at home in Mezbizh. That little town so distant from Warsaw and yet so near was the place to which my childish imagination went on many journeys. Every step taken on the way was an answer to a prayer, and every stone was a memory of a marvel. For most of the wondrous deeds my father told about either happened in Mezbizh or were inspired by those mysterious men who lived there.

The earliest fascination I can recall is associated with the Baal Shem, whose parables disclosed some of the first insights I gained as a child. He remained a model too sublime to follow yet too overwhelming to ignore.

It was in my ninth year that the presence of Reb Menahem Mendl of Kotzk, known as the Kotzker, entered my life. Since then he has remained a steady companion and a haunting challenge. Although he often stunted me, he also urged me to confront perplexities that I might have preferred to evade.

Years later I realized that, in being guided by both the Baal Shem Tov and the Kotzker, I had allowed two forces to carry on a struggle within me. One was occasionally mightier than the other. But who was to prevail, which was to be my guide? Both spoke convincingly, and each proved right on one level yet questionable on another.

In a very strange way, I found my soul at home with the Baal Shem but driven by the Kotzker. Was it good to live with one's heart torn between the joy of Mezbizh and the anxiety of Kotzk? To live both in awe and consternation, in fervor and horror, with my conscience on mercy and my eyes on Auschwitz, wavering between exaltation and dismay? Was this a life a man would choose to live? I had no choice: my heart was in Mezbizh, my mind in Kotzk.

I was taught about inexhaustible mines of meaning by the Baal Shem; from the Kotzker I learned to detect immense mountains of absurdity standing in the way. The one taught me song, the other — silence. The one reminded me that there could be a heaven on earth, the other shocked me into discovering hell in the alleged heavenly places in our world.

The Baal Shem made dark hours luminous; the Kotzker eased wretchedness and desolation by forewarnings, by premonitions. The Kotzker restricted me, debunked cherished attitudes. From the Baal Shem I received the gifts of elasticity in adapting to contradictory conditions.

The Baal Shem dwelled in my life like a lamp, while the Kotzker struck like lightning. To be sure, lightning is more authentic. Yet one can trust a lamp, put confidence in it; one can live in peace with a lamp.

The Baal Shem gave me wings; the Kotzker encircled me with chains. I never had the courage to break the chains and entered into joys with my shortcomings in mind. I owe intoxication to the Baal Shem, to the Kotzker the blessings of humiliation.

The Kotzker's presence recalls the nightmare of mendacity. The presence of Baal Shem is an assurance that falsehood dissolves into compassion through the power of love. The Baal Shem suspends sadness; the Kotzker enhances it. The Baal Shem helped me to refine my sense of immediate mystery; the Kotzker warned me of the constant peril of forfeiting authenticity.

Honesty, authenticity, integrity without love may lead to the ruin of others, of oneself, or both. On the other hand, love, fervor, or exaltation alone may seduce us into living in a fool's Paradise — a wise man's hell.   — *PFT,* xiii–xv

IN PRAISE OF STRICT JUSTICE

According to the Midrash, God first intended to rule with stern justice the world He created. Realizing, however, that it would not endure, He gave precedence to divine mercy, allying it with divine justice.

An old tradition maintains that the Holy One, blessed be He, prays. What kind of prayer? Abba Arika (Rab), a celebrated sage who died in 247, suggested the following:

> May it be My will that My mercy may suppress My anger, that My mercy may prevail over My other attributes, so that I may deal with My children in the attribute of mercy and on their behalf stop short of the limit of stern justice.

Mercy rather than justice is regarded as the outstanding attribute of God. The rabbis speak of the "thirteen attributes of compassion" (Exodus 34:6–7). While one of the most often used synonyms for God is "Compassionate One" (*Rahmana*), no synonym has been coined to denote the Lord as dispenser of justice.

The Kotzker, however, demurred. He considered mercy an attenuation of Truth. To show mercy means to compromise with evil and to come to terms with delinquency. If the world were conducted according to the principle of Truth, justice, not mercy, would be administered.

Reb Mendl cited a rabbinic thesis that the greatness of God, the King of Kings, is disclosed in His being a lover of Justice (Psalm 99:4). This was his will: to favor man with benefits based on justice because he deserved them. God should not have to resort to mercy and bestow the good undeservedly. In rabbinic tradition, the ineffable Name, "the Lord," denotes the attribute of mercy, while the word "God" (*elohim*) signifies justice.

In this sense, too, the Kotzker explained the words of the Psalmist as a prayer for justice rather than mercy. "My soul thirsts for God.... When shall I come and behold the face of God" (Psalm 42:3). Consistent in his commitment to Truth as the supreme standard for right and wrong, the Kotzker felt that to accept mercy as the supreme standard was a sign of weakness. Justice is the way of Truth.

The dichotomy between Truth and mercy agonized Reb Shneur Zalman of Laydy, founder of the Habad Hasidism, during his last hours on earth. In a brief essay written shortly before he died, he concluded that the world was created on the principle of "mercy devoid (or in disregard) of Truth." Therefore, since most of men's deeds are false, it is impossible to carry out an act of mercy and an act of truth simultaneously. In a world of falsehood, human mercy is tainted with falsehood; only the Torah is Truth.

Even exalted people often ignored the Truth, wrote Reb Shneur Zalman, for this was "a world of lies and mercies." Did he then equate mercies with lies? And did the Kotzker give no thought to God's love and mercy? Did he solely emphasize man's falsehood and corruption?

It is natural to feel uncomfortable when confronted with such austerity. Yet a sense of comfort is no standard for Truth. It is precisely the one-sided emphasis upon God's love and mercy that stands in need of a corrective. We must be reminded that the God of the Bible is both Judge and Father, severe as well as compassionate.

The Kotzker's thought does not offer a pleasing interpretation of man. Its core is an urgent call for self-examination, a critical surveying of our claims, our pride, a call for candor and humility. The disasters Jews have experienced in the twentieth century substantiate the Kotzker's admonitions against man's unreliability, revealing the insecurity of freedom. His incisive insights should open our eyes to inauthenticity in the sphere of religion, to the outright deceptions in politics and social relations and in institutional operations. *—PFT,* 131–33

RELIGIOUS TRUTH MUST BE LIVED

Religious truth must be lived. A law unrelated to life is both futile and fatal to faith. Rigidity and love of life cannot always be reconciled. If, as rabbinic authorities have declared, the aim of fulfilling the Law is in the ennoblement of the person, Jewish jurisdiction should take this into account.

If he were alive today, the Kotzker would look aghast at the replacement of spirituality by aesthetics, spontaneity by decorum. Like Kierkegaard, he would vehemently condemn an aesthetic concept of Judaism acted out in customs, ceremonies, sentimental celebrations, and polished oratory, as well as in decorative representations of God in terms of grandiose temples. He would also reject the reduction of Judaism to an outward compliance with ritual laws, strict observance mingled with dishonesty, the pedantic performance of rituals as a form of opportunism.

The Kotzker would call upon us to be uneasy about our situation, to feel ashamed of our peace of mind, of our spiritual stagnation. One's integrity must constantly be examined. In his view, self-assurance, smug certainty of one's honesty was as objectionable as brazen dishonesty. A moderately clean heart was like a moderately foul egg. Lukewarm Judaism would be as effective in purging our character as a lukewarm furnace in melting steel.

Gone for our time is the sweetness of faith. It has ceased to come to us as a gift. It requires "blood, sweat, and tears." We are frightened by a world that God may be ready to abandon. What a nightmare to live in a cosmic lie, in an absurdity that makes pretensions to beauty.

The predicament of contemporary man is grave. We seem to be destined either for a new mutation or for destruction. Some of the Kotzker's and Kierkegaard's insights may help us tap sources for a renewal of faith.

It seems as if Reb Mendl's unfettered soul anticipated ineluctable disasters that sheer mendacity was to incite and to abet. To the gloom that this realization cast upon him was added the knowledge that people refused to listen to a message of dismay. He faced defection, misinterpretations. Indeed, the disciple in whom he had placed the greatest confidence, from whom he had expected the most, and to whom he entrusted the spiritual training of the novices who came to Kotzk, defected, left his master, and established a school of his own, in sharp opposition to his mentor.

The Kotzker could not anticipate the disaster that befell his people during the Holocaust. He did not deal with the political situation of the Jews or with the phenomenon of anti-Semitism. Nevertheless, he seems to have had a haunting awareness of the terrible danger of human cruelty. He may not have analyzed the dynamic nature of persecution, yet he was profoundly aware that in a world of lies the demonic had a free reign. Had he been alive in the 1940s the Holocaust would not have come as a surprise to his soul.

Indeed, when human beings establish a modus vivendi on the basis of mendacity, the world can turn into a nightmare. This may explain the obsessive preoccupation with falsehood in the Kotzker's thinking. For the Holocaust did not take place suddenly. It was in the making for several generations. It had its origin in a lie: that the Jew was responsible for all social ills, for all personal frustrations. Decimate the Jews and all problems would be solved.

The Holocaust was initiated by demonic thoughts, savage words. What is the state of mankind today? Has the mind been purged, have the words been cleansed of corrupt deceit? How shall we prevent genocide in the years to come? Has mankind become less cruel, less callous?

To understand the Kotzker or Kierkegaard, we must learn to abandon the view that religion is simply morality tinged with emotion. It is above all a world of its own, a private, secret realm of relationships between God and man. The supreme rule in this world is not that beauty should reign supreme but Truth: a precarious virtue, indeed; yet only in Truth can exaltation come to pass, an exaltation that raises the whole man to the level of the divine.

Kierkegaard taught that the religious stage rose beyond the ethical and that the two stages were sometimes irreconcilable.

As a classical example, he cited the story of Abraham's readiness to offer Isaac as a sacrifice. The Kotzker came close to this view. Although he maintained that religious existence could not be fully realized without ritual and ethical content, the demands he made on his disciples implied a clear disregard of their moral obligations toward their families.

Kierkegaard wrote in his journal, "My life will cry out after my death." Decades later the Western world began to hear his cry. Similarly, the Kotzker's cry of alarm may now begin to be heard.

If all agony were kept alive in memory, if all turmoil were told, who could endure tranquility? Reb Mendl was one of those who stressed the speciousness of tranquility. He chased away all comfort, all calm.

In a world that contains so much sham, the Kotzker continues to stand before us as a soul aflame with passion for God, determined to let nothing stand between him and his Maker. In the nineteenth century he was a towering figure, in solitary misery as in grandeur. Yet his spirit, his accent are those of the post-Auschwitz era.

We recall him still, Reb Mendl of Kotzk. He has not fled from us by dying. Somehow his lightning persists. His words throw flames whenever they come into our orbit. They burn. Who can bear them? Yet many of us shall thereby shed our masks, our pretensions and jealousies, our distorted notions, and the messianic redemption may approach its beginning.

What did the Kotzker leave behind? He published no books, left no records; what he wrote he burned. Yet he taught us never to say farewell to Truth; for God laughs at those who think that falseness is inevitable. He also enabled us to face wretchedness and survive. For Truth is alive, dwelling somewhere, never weary. And all of mankind is needed to liberate it.

—*PFT,* 320–23

FROM THE POINT OF VIEW OF GOD

I came with great hunger to the University of Berlin to study philosophy. I looked for a system of thought, for the depth of the spirit, for the meaning of existence. Erudite and profound scholars gave courses in logic, epistemology, esthetics, ethics, and metaphysics. They opened the gates of the history of philosophy. I was exposed to the austere discipline of unremitting inquiry and self-criticism. I communed with the thinkers of the past who knew how to meet intellectual adversity with fortitude and learned to dedicate myself to the examination of basic premises at the risk of failure.

Yet, in spite of the intellectual power and honesty which I was privileged to witness, I became increasingly aware of the gulf that separated my views from those held at the university. I had come with a sense of anxiety: How can I rationally find a way where ultimate meaning lies, a way of living where one would never miss a reference to supreme significance? Why am I here at all, and what is my purpose? I did not even know how to phrase my concern. But to my teachers that was a question unworthy of philosophical analysis.

I realized my teachers were prisoners of a Greek-German way of thinking. They were fettered in categories which presupposed certain metaphysical assumptions which could never be proved. The questions I was moved by could not even be adequately phrased in categories of their thinking.

My assumption was: man's dignity consists in his having been created in the likeness of God. My question was: how must man, a being who is in essence the image of God, think, feel, and act? To them, religion was a feeling. To me, religion included the insights of the Torah, which is a vision of man from the point of view of God. They spoke of God from the point of view of man. To them God was an idea, a postulate of reason. They granted Him the status of being a logical possibility. But to assume that He had existence would have been a crime against epistemology.

The problem to my professors was how to be good. In my ears the question rang: how to be holy. At the time I realized: there is much that philosophy could learn from Jewish life. To the philosophers: the idea of the good was the most exalted idea, the ultimate idea. To Judaism the idea of the good is penultimate. It cannot exist without the holy. The good is the base, the holy is the summit. Man cannot be good unless he strives to be holy.

To have an idea of the good is not the same as living by the insight, *Blessed is the man who does not forget Thee.*

I did not come to the university because I did not know the idea of the good, but to learn why the idea of the good is valid, why and whether values had meaning. Yet I discovered that values sweet to taste proved sour in analysis; the prototypes were firm, the models flabby. Must speculation and existence remain like two infinite parallel lines that never meet? Or perhaps this impossibility of juncture is the result of the fact that our speculation suffers from what is called in astronomy a parallax, from the apparent displacement of the object, caused by the actual change of our point of observation?

In those months in Berlin I went through moments of profound bitterness. I felt very much alone with my own problems and anxieties. I walked alone in the evenings through the magnificent streets of Berlin. I admired the solidity of its architecture, the overwhelming drive and power of a dynamic civilization. There were concerts, theaters, and lectures by famous scholars about the latest theories and inventions, and I was pondering whether to go to the new Max Reinhardt play or to a lecture about the theory of relativity.

Suddenly I noticed the sun had gone down; evening had arrived.

From what time may one recite the Shema in the evening?

I had forgotten God — I had forgotten Sinai — I had forgotten that sunset is my business — that my task is "to restore the world to the kingship of the Lord."

So I began to utter the words of the evening prayer.

Blessed art thou, Lord our God,
King of the universe,
who by His word brings on the evenings....

And Goethe's famous poem rang in my ear:

Ueber allen Gipfeln ist Ruh'
O'er all the hilltops is quiet now.

No, that was pagan thinking. To the pagan eye the mystery of life is *Ruh'*, death, oblivion. To us Jews, there is meaning beyond the mystery. We would say

O'er all the hilltops is the word of God.

The meaning of life is to do His will.... And I uttered the words,

Who by His word brings on the evenings.

And His love is manifested in His teaching us Torah, precepts, laws:

Ueber allen Gipfeln is God's love for man —.

Thou hast loved the house of Israel with everlasting love.
Thou hast taught us Torah, mitzvot, laws, rules....

How much guidance, how many ultimate insights are found in our liturgy.

How grateful I am to God that there is a duty to worship, a law to remind my distraught mind that it is time to think of God, time to disregard my ego for at least a moment! It is such happiness to belong to an order of the divine will.

I am not always in a mood to pray. I do not always have the vision and the strength to say a word in the presence of God. But when I am weak, it is the law that gives me strength; when my vision is dim, it is duty that gives me insight.

Indeed, there is something which is far greater than my desire to pray, namely, God's desire that I pray. There is something which is far greater than my will to believe, namely, God's will that I believe. How insignificant is my praying in the midst of a cosmic process! Unless it is the will of God that I pray, how ludicrous is it to pray.

On that evening in the streets of Berlin, I was not in a mood to pray. My heart was heavy; my soul was sad. It was difficult for the lofty words of prayer to break through the dark clouds of my inner life.

But how would I dare not to *pray*? How would I dare to miss an evening prayer? "Out of *emah,* out of fear of God do we read the *Shema*" (*me-emah-thai,* the first word of the tractate *Berachoth,* Rabbi Levi Yizhak).

The following morning I awoke in my student room. Now the magnificent achievements in the field of physiology and psychology have, of course, not diminished, but rather increased my sense of wonder for the human body and soul. And so I prayed

Blessed be Thou ... who hast formed man in wisdom. ...
My God, the soul which Thou hast placed within me is
pure. ...

Yet how am I going to keep my soul clean?

The most important problem which a human being must face daily is: How to maintain one's integrity in a world where power, success, and money are valued above all else? How to remain clean amid the mud of falsehood and malice that soil our society?

The soul is clean, but within it resides a power for evil, "a strange god," that "seeks constantly to get the upper hand over man and to kill him; and if God did not help him, he could not resist it, as it is said, 'the wicked watches the righteous, and seeks to slay him.' "

Every morning I take a piece of cloth — neither elegant nor solemn, of no particular esthetic beauty, a prayer-shawl, wrap myself in it and say:

How precious is Thy kindness, O God! The children of man take refuge in the shadow of Thy wings. They have their fill of the choice food of Thy house, and Thou givest them drink of Thy stream of delights. For with Thee is the fountain of life; by Thy light do we see light. Continue Thy kindness to those who know Thee, and Thy righteousness to the upright in heart.

But, then, I ask myself: Have I got a right to take my refuge in Him? to drink of the stream of His delights? to expect Him to continue His kindness? But God wants me to be close to Him, even to bind every morning His word as a sign on my hand, and between my eyes. I would remind myself of the word that God spoke to *me* through His prophet Hosea: "I will betroth you unto Me forever; I will betroth you unto Me in righteousness and in justice, in kindness and in mercy. I will betroth you unto Me in faithfulness; and you shall know the Lord" (Hosea 2:21–22). It is an act of betrothal, a promise to marry.... It is an act of God, falling in love with His people. But the engagement depends on righteousness, justice, kindness, mercy.

Why did I decide to take religious observance seriously in spite of the numerous perplexities in which I became enmeshed?

Why did I pray, although I was not in a mood to pray? And why was I able to pray in spite of being unprepared to pray? What was my situation after the reminder to pray the evening prayer struck my mind? The duty to worship stood as a thought of ineffable meaning; doubt, the voice of disbelief, was ready to challenge it. But where should the engagement take place? In an act of reflection the duty to worship is a mere thought, timid, frail, a mere shadow of reality, while the voice of disbelief is a power, well-armed with the weight of inertia and the preference for abstention. In such an engagement prayer would be fought *in absentia,* and the issue would be decided without actually joining the battle. It was fair, therefore, to give the weaker rival a chance: to pray first, to fight later.

I realized that just as you cannot study philosophy through praying, you cannot study prayer through philosophizing. And what applies to prayer is true in regard to the essentials of Jewish observance.

What I wanted to avoid was not only the failure to pray to God during a whole evening of my life but *the loss of the whole,* the loss of belonging to the spiritual order of Jewish living. It is true that some people are so busy with collecting shreds and patches of the law that they hardly think of weaving the pattern of the whole. But there is also the danger of being so enchanted by the whole as to lose sight of the detail. It became increasingly clear to me that the order of Jewish living is meant to be, not a set of rituals, but an order of all man's existence, shaping all his traits, interests and, dispositions; "not so much the performance of single acts, the taking of a step now and then, as the pursuit of a way, being on the way; not so much the acts of fulfilling as the state of being committed to the task, the belonging to an order in which single deeds, aggregates of religious feeling, sporadic sentiments, moral episodes become a part of a complete pattern" (*MNA,* 270).

The ineffable Name, we have forgotten how to pronounce it. We have almost forgotten how to spell it. We may totally forget how to recognize it.   —*MQG,* 94–100

SOME OF US BLUSH

God is unwilling to be alone, and man cannot forever remain impervious to what He longs to show. Those of us who cannot keep their striving back find themselves at times within the sight of the unseen and become aglow with its rays. Some of us blush; others wear a mask. Faith is a blush in the presence of God.

Some of us blush, others wear a mask which veils spontaneous sensitivity to the holy ineffable dimension of reality. We all wear so much mental make-up, we have almost forfeited our face. But faith only comes when we stand face to face — the ineffable in us with the ineffable beyond us — suffer ourselves to be seen, to commune, to receive a ray and to reflect it. But to do that the soul must be alive within the mind.

Responsiveness to God cannot be copied; it must be original with every soul. Even the meaning of the divine is not grasped when imposed by a doctrine, when accepted by hearsay. It only enters our vision when leaping like a spark from the anvil of the mind, hammered and beaten upon by trembling awe.

Those who search after Him in abstractions will miss Him. He is not a lost pearl at the bottom of the mind, to be found when diving in the waves of argument. The greatest is never that which you expect.

It is in our ability to grasp Him that we come closest to Him. The existence of God is not real because it is conceivable; it is conceivable because it is real. And real it is to him who learns to live in tremor and awe for no purpose, for no reward; who abides in tremor and awe because he could not do otherwise; who lives in the awareness of the ineffable, even though it may seem foolish, futile, and improper.

Thinking about God as a hobby, as a part-time occupation, will fail even to set forth the issue. For what is the issue in which we are involved? Is it curiosity of the kind we entertain when being inquisitive about the nature of electronics? Electronics does not ask anything of us, while the beginning of what God means is the awareness of our being committed to Him.

God is not an explanation of the world's enigmas or a guarantee of our salvation. He is an eternal challenge, an urgent demand. He is not a problem to be solved but a question addressed to us as individuals, as nations, as mankind.

God is of no importance unless He is of supreme importance, which means a deep certainty that it is better to be defeated with Him than be victorious without Him.

The man who lives by his faith is he who — even if scholars
the world over should proclaim, if all mankind by an overwhelming majority of votes should endorse, and if experiments,
which at times adapt themselves to man's favorite theories,
should corroborate that there is no God — would rather suffer at the hands of reason than accept his own reason as an
idol; who would grieve, but neither totter nor betray the dignity
of his sense of inadequacy in the presence of the ineffable. For
faith is an earnest we hold till the hour of passing away, not
to be redeemed by a doctrine or even exchanged for insights.
What God means is expressed in the words: "For Thy kindness
is better than life" (Psalm 63:4). God is He whose regard for
me I value more than life.

Faith is not captured in observing events in the physical
world that deviate from the known laws of nature. Of what
avail are miracles, with our senses unreliable, with our knowledge incomplete? Faith precedes any palpable experience, rather
than derives from it. Without possessing faith, no experience
will communicate to us religious significance.

It says in the Song of Songs: "As an apple tree among the
trees of the wood" (2:3). Rabbi Aha ben Zeira made a compar-
ison: "The apple tree brings out its blossom before its leaves,
so Israel in Egypt had achieved faith even before they perceived
the message of redemption, as it says: 'And the people believed;
and they heard that the Lord had remembered' (Exodus 4:31)"
(Midrash Haxita 2, 10).

A saying of Rabbi Isaac Meir of Ger may illustrate what
we mean. Commenting on the verse: "And Israel saw the great
work which the Lord did upon the Egyptians, and the people
feared the Lord; and they had faith in the Lord, and in His ser-
vant Moses" (Exodus 14:31), he remarked: "Although they saw
the miracles with their own eyes, they were still in need of faith,
because faith is superior to sight; with faith you see more than
with your eyes."   — MNA, 91–93

MAN'S RELEVANCE TO GOD

The theology of pathos brings about a shift in the understanding of man's ultimate problems. The prophet does not see the human situation in and by itself. The predicament of man is a predicament of God Who has a stake in the human situation. The life of sin is more than a failure of man; it is a frustration to God. Thus, man's alienation from God is not the ultimate fact by which to measure man's situation. The divine pathos, the fact of God's participation in the predicament of man, is the elemental fact.

The essential meaning of pathos is, therefore, not to be seen in its psychological denotation, as standing for a state of the soul, but in its theological connotation, signifying God as involved in history. He is engaged to Israel — and has a stake in its destiny. The profundity of this insight can be sensed only in the light of the prophet's awareness of the mystery and transcendence of God. For the biblical understanding of history, the idea of pathos is as central as the idea of man being an image of God is for the understanding of creation.

The biblical writers were aware of the paradox involved in God's relation to man. "Behold, to the Lord your God belong heaven and the heaven of heavens, the earth with all that is in it; yet the Lord set His heart in love upon your fathers and chose their descendants after them, you above all peoples, as at this day" (Deuteronomy 10:14–15).

Never in history has man been taken as seriously as in prophetic thinking. Man is not only an image of God; he is a perpetual concern of God. The idea of pathos adds a new dimension to human existence. Whatever man does affects not only his own life; but also the life of God insofar as it is directed to man. The import of man raises him beyond the level of mere creature. He is a consort, a partner, a factor in the life of God.

—*Prophets,* 291–92

WHAT TO DO WITH WONDER

The beginning of faith is not a feeling for the mystery of living or a sense of awe, wonder, or fear. The root of religion is the question what to do with the feeling for the mystery of living, what to do with awe, wonder, or fear. Religion, the end of isolation, begins with a consciousness that something is asked of us. It is in that tense, eternal asking in which the soul is caught and in which man's answer is elicited.

Wonder is not a state of esthetic enjoyment. Endless wonder is endless tension, a situation in which we are shocked at the inadequacy of our awe, at the weakness of our shock, as well as the state of being asked the ultimate question.

Endless wonder unlocks an innate sense of indebtedness. Within our awe there is no place for self-assertion. Within our awe we only know that all we own we owe. The world consists, not of things, but of tasks. Wonder is the state of our being asked. The ineffable is a question addressed to us.

All that is left to us is a choice — to answer or to refuse to answer. Yet the more deeply we listen, the more we become stripped of the arrogance and callousness which alone would enable us to refuse. We carry a load of marvel, wishing to exchange it for the simplicity of knowing what to live for, a load which we can never lay down nor continue to carry not knowing where.

At the moment in which a fire bursts forth, threatening to destroy one's home, a person does not pause to investigate whether the danger he faces is real or a figment of his imagination. Such a moment is not the time to inquire into the chemical principle of combustion or into the question of who is to blame for the outbreak of the fire. The ultimate question, when bursting forth in our souls, is too startling, too heavily laden with unutterable wonder to be an academic question, to be equally suspended between yes and no. Such a moment is not the time to throw doubts upon the reason for the rise of the question.

— *MNA*, 68–69

OUR DESTINY IS TO AID

The greatest problem is not how to continue but how to exalt our existence. They cry for a life beyond the grave is presumptuous, if there is no cry for eternal life prior to our descending to the grave. Eternity is not perpetual future but perpetual presence. He has planted in us the seed of eternal life. The world to come is not only a hereafter but also a *herenow*.

Our greatest problem is not how to continue but how to return. "How can I repay unto the Lord all his bountiful dealings with me?" (Psalm 116:12). When life is an answer, death is a homecoming. "Precious in the sight of the Lord is the death of his saints" (Psalm 116:14). For our greatest problem is but a resonance of God's concern: How can I repay unto man all his bountiful dealings with me? "For the mercy of God endureth forever."

This is the meaning of existence: to reconcile liberty with service, the passing with the lasting, to weave the threads of temporality into the fabric of eternity.

The deepest wisdom man can attain is to know that his destiny is to aid, to serve. We have to conquer in order to succumb; we have to acquire in order to give away; we have to triumph in order to be overwhelmed. Man has to understand in order to believe, to know in order to accept. The aspiration is to obtain; the perfection is to dispense. This is the meaning of death: the ultimate self-dedication to the divine. Death so understood will not be distorted by the craving for immortality, for this act of giving away is reciprocity on man's part for God's gift of life. For the pious man it is a privilege to die.   —*MNA, 295–96*

MODERN SPIRITUAL MASTERS
Robert Ellsberg, Series Editor

Already published:

Dietrich Bonhoeffer (edited by Robert Coles)

Simone Weil (edited by Eric O. Springsted)

Henri Nouwen (edited by Robert A. Jonas)

Pierre Teilhard de Chardin (edited by Ursula King)

Anthony de Mello (edited by William Dych, S.J.)

Charles de Foucauld (edited by Robert Ellsberg)

Oscar Romero (by Marie Dennis, Rennie Golden, and Scott Wright)

Eberhard Arnold (edited by Johann Christoph Arnold)

Thomas Merton (edited by Christine M. Bochen)

Thich Nhat Hanh (edited by Robert Ellsberg)

Rufus Jones (edited by Kerry Walters)

Mother Teresa (edited by Jean Maalouf)

Edith Stein (edited by John Sullivan, O.C.D.)

John Main (edited by Laurence Freeman)

Mohandas Gandhi (edited by John Dear)

Mother Maria Skobtsova (introduction by Jim Forest)

Evelyn Underhill (edited by Emilie Griffin)

St. Thérèse of Lisieux (edited by Mary Frohlich)

Flannery O'Connor (edited by Robert Ellsberg)

Clarence Jordan (edited by Joyce Hollyday)

G. K. Chesterton (edited by William Griffin)

Alfred Delp, S.J. (introduction by Thomas Merton)

Bede Griffiths (edited by Thomas Matus)

Karl Rahner (edited by Philip Endean)

Sadhu Sundar Singh (edited by Charles E. Moore)

Pedro Arrupe (edited by Kevin F. Burke, S.J.)

Romano Guardini (edited by Robert A. Krieg)
Albert Schweitzer (edited by James Brabazon)
Caryll Houselander (edited by Wendy M. Wright)
Brother Roger of Taizé (edited by Marcello Fidanzio)
Dorothee Soelle (edited by Dianne L. Oliver)
Leo Tolstoy (edited by Charles E. Moore)
Howard Thurman (edited by Luther E. Smith, Jr.)
Swami Abhishiktananda (edited by Shirley du Boulay)
Carlo Carretto (edited by Robert Ellsberg)
John XXIII (edited by Jean Maalouf)
Jean Vanier (edited by Carolyn Whitney-Brown)
The Dalai Lama (edited by Thomas A. Forsthoefel)
Catherine de Hueck Doherty (edited by David Meconi, S.J.)
Dom Helder Camara (edited by Francis McDonagh)
Daniel Berrigan (edited by John Dear)
Etty Hillesum (edited by Annemarie S. Kidder)
Virgilio Elizondo (edited by Timothy Matovina)
Metropolitan Anthony of Sourozh (edited by Gillian Crow)
David Steindl-Rast (edited by Clare Hallward)
Frank Sheed and Maisie Ward (edited by David Meconi)